FAITH TRIUMPHANT

Books by the same author

MASON OF KWANGCHOW CIM, 1929
GEORGE KING—MEDICAL EVANGELIST CIM, 1930
CHINA CALLING CIM, 1936
IF WE BELIEVE IVF, 1952
  Second edition: FAITH'S UNCLAIMED INHERITANCE IVF, 1961
AMY CARMICHAEL OF DOHNAVUR SPCK, 1953
LIVING YOUR LIFE Falcon Press, 1966
THE FIRE BURNS ON (Editor) CIM–OMF, 1965

FAITH TRIUMPHANT

An Anthology of Verse

by

FRANK HOUGHTON

1894-1972

Bishop of East Szechwan

General Director of the China Inland Mission

OMF BOOKS ◊ LONDON

First published .. .. *June 1973*

ISBN 85363 089 5 (*paperback*)
ISBN 85363 091 7 (*casebound*)

Made in Great Britain
Published by OMF Books,
Newington Green, London, N16 9QD
and printed by The Camelot Press Ltd,
London and Southampton

CONTENTS

One eager hope, one passionate desire,
One grand, all-unifying aim—
Albeit in doubt's dark night or pain's fierce fire—
Let me bring glory to His Name!

"Always"—not only when to heedless ears
The gracious Voice sounds close beside,
But through the slow unfolding of the years,
Let Jesus Christ be magnified!

And since glib-tongued too lightly we aspire
In unconsidered prayer and vow,
Here in this hour, lest love's resolve should tire,
I pray, "As always, Lord, so now"!

FOREWORD

By Canon T. G. Mohan

Many who knew Bishop Frank Houghton and rejoice to sing his hymns which have become the Church's possession, may not know of the wealth of his verse which has not hitherto been published in a single volume. This anthology will be eagerly read by those whose spiritual life has already been enriched by his writings, and by the example of his consecrated life.

As a boy he began the lifelong habit of expressing his inmost relationship with the Lord in verse, and thus early revealed a gift which he has always used to glorify the Lord. In these poems he expresses the complete and utter dedication of his whole life to his Saviour. He reveals his own intimate daily walk with the Lord Jesus, his absolute trust and confidence through every circumstance, his joyful acceptance of His will for good or ill, and his desire to serve Him unreservedly to his life's end.

To read this anthology is a deeply moving experience. It includes a brief review of Frank Houghton's life, which shows this gentle, kindly, sensitive man to be a man of great courage, fearless and composed in the presence of dangers which threatened life itself. It also provides the background against which the verse becomes meaningful. In addition there are footnotes in the text which relate the poems to the circumstances in which they were written.

Here is a book which does not give to a man the glory which belongs to the Lord alone, but through the man it magnifies the Lord whose glory was his own first desire. I am greatly privileged to be asked to write this Foreword, and I pray that *Faith Triumphant* may help many to a deeper trust and dedication to our Lord Jesus Christ.

PREFACE

It is hard to think of Bishop Houghton apart from his hymns, his poems and his music. They were his constant companions. The examples given in this volume reveal the youth and the man, the disciple and the leader, to be transparently the worshipping follower of the One he loved and the true exemplar of the faith he encouraged in his fellow Christians. They reveal a spiritual pilgrimage, a soul's deepening experience of God and His faithfulness, of dedication to his fight with the powers of darkness, and of the triumphs of truth and trust as he experienced more of the indwelling of Christ Himself.

Frank Houghton's verse becomes more meaningful when the occasion of its inspiration is known. Not every setting has, however, been discovered. Whenever possible a few notes have been given, but a characteristic of many of these poems is their relevance to very different circumstances from those that prompted them. This makes them all the more appropriate to be shared with a wider world of readers than the extensive circle of friends and acquaintances who "thank God upon every remembrance" of Frank Houghton's life.

A chronological arrangement has been adopted to follow the sequence of historical events and to allow the earlier verse to stand in true perspective.

Already several of his hymns and choruses have become part of the heritage of the Church; other verse in this anthology may find its place in general use when the power of its depth with simplicity is better appreciated.

In this brief volume no attempt is made to assess the importance of the man or the quality of his poetry. Nor is it a study of his personality. It is enough, so soon after his departure, to pay tribute to the grace of God revealed in him.

Frank Houghton often used to quote the words of Dr. James Denney:

> No one can bear witness to Christ and himself at the same time. No one can give the impression that he is clever and that Christ is mighty to save. The impression on the Jewish Council was that Peter and John were not clever, but they had been with Jesus.

This is what Frank would remind us regarding the publication of his poems.

A. J. B.

Frank Houghton and his Verse

Frank Houghton's lifelong aim and ambition, consciously adopted when still a boy, was to glorify God in all that he said and did. He would not have wished even this brief introduction to an anthology of his verse to be given to adulation. "I would be nothing—all things for Thy sake," he wrote at seventeen. As an indication, however, of what God can do through a consecrated soul, an outline of his life and Christian experience may be useful.

Frank was born on April 24th, 1894, at Stafford, where his father, the Rev. Thomas Houghton, was still a curate. He was the fourth of eight children, of whom four were boys and four girls. Moreover, four besides himself became missionaries overseas: Eileen and Alfred (Canon A. T. Houghton) in Burma under the Bible Churchmen's Missionary Society, and Stanley and Freda with the China Inland Mission.

SCHOOLDAYS

The earliest examples of verse preserved by Frank's brothers and sisters were written in 1907–11 when he was thirteen to seventeen years of age. There is in them the germ of his later gift, although, until he developed his own confident style, some of them reflect the poetic diet of the time on which he was clearly being fed. They hailed the birthdays of his family in Edwardian rhetoric and sentiment and, without hypocrisy, flights of piety which echo contemporary fashion. But "nonsense rhymes" and healthy fun also abound to reveal the bubbling spirit that remained with him throughout life.

To Lydia, for her thirteenth birthday on August 29th, 1911, for example:

It's ridiculous, really, to hope for a line
From a bed-ridden fellow like me,
But yet I suppose I must send you this sign
That my true-hearted love you may see.

Of course I regret that the pudding's not here,
But waiting at home for consumption,
But yet, if it came, it would soon disappear,
For we eat without judgment or gumption.

You can easily tell, if your brain's not unsound
Without any great perspicacity,
That a rhyme for "consumption" was not to be found
Without straining the bonds of veracity.

I have nothing to say, and my brain's in a whirl,
So I simply repeat my good wishes:
If you think this is bosh, like a sensible girl,
Let it go to be food for the fishes!

And to Freda, on her ninth birthday, at the end of December, in the same year:

Her curls were dark, as black as jet,
That day, nine years ago,
She has them still, though they are brown
Which now around her blow.

And I remember, too, the day
When first I saw her smile
(Although she poured forth tears enough
To overflow the Nile).

A slight exaggeration? Yes!
Perhaps you may be right;
But babies often squeal you know,
From morning until night.

Frank knew and loved the Saviour from early childhood and came to honour Him as Lord before his confirmation on April 8th, 1908, when he was not yet fourteen. He was already writing serious poetry like "The Night is Dark" (No. 1), and his carol, "Loud songs of exultation raise" (No. 2) was included in the "Beaufort Hymnal", a family manuscript hymn-book compiled by Eileen and Alfred Houghton in 1910 when Frank was sixteen. A Coronation Hymn which he wrote for King George V and Queen Mary's coronation in 1911 was printed and used in the Kensington Episcopal Chapel, Bath, (No. 7).

In the same year he was saved from drowning, but only just in time, for he was already unconscious. Frank and Alfred (later always known as "Tim"), were bathing at low tide at Boscombe, though neither could swim, when the in-coming tide cut them off and engulfed them about a hundred yards from the shore. Their sisters on the beach heard their cries, and Eileen rushed fully clothed to the rescue. Thinking that she was trying to commit suicide, a man followed her and so was there to dive and look for the boys. He dragged Alfred out by the hair and brought him ashore. It was not till later that two other men, urgently persuaded by the sisters, also went out and, finding Frank under water, brought him in. Both boys were unconscious but were resuscitated by prolonged artificial respiration, Frank as long as twenty minutes after his brother. Not surprisingly, that night, when lying still exhausted in bed, both realized that God had given them back their lives that they might spend them in His service (No. 9). In *Daily Light* the same evening they read from Psalm 40.2, 3, "He brought me up out of an horrible pit, out of the miry clay, and set my feet upon a rock, and established my goings. And he hath put a new song in my mouth, even praise to our God". There is no doubt that this experience had a profound effect on the missionary careers of both brothers.

Frank's reference to being "bed-ridden", in his Poem for Lydia, dated August 29th, 1911, four days after his miraculous escape, refers to the fact that he had some lung congestion which prevented him from going back to school at the end of the summer holidays. Physically he was never very robust and was unable to play football, but his exuberant spirits made up for any lack of athletic ability and his closest friends were among those who possessed the physical strength that he lacked.

At Clarence School, in Weston-super-Mare, his Christian testimony was clear and positive, expressed sometimes in poems in the school magazine, *The Clarencian*, together with verse of a secular nature. But so facile was he in rhyme and rhythm and skit that on one occasion, when some topical verse of his recited in a school concert drew an insistent demand for an encore, the headmaster blithely stated that Frank would oblige towards the end of the concert. On the spur of the moment he composed some more verses which were received with rapturous applause.

The introspective, contemplative poems of his teenage years throw light upon the spiritual battles through which he was passing, and so provide a backdrop against which his more mature and

Christocentric verse can be judged—after he had won his victory over temptations to relax his dedication to Christ and pursue his own life and ambitions (No. 8):

Oh, that I could know
The future, and the part I have to play.

It is understandable that clichés of poetic phraseology in an age of conventionalism are borrowed freely.

Those hopes of pow'r and greatness that hold sway
Within my breast, will on some far-off day
Be gratified, e'en here on earth below!

But "the spontaneous overflow of powerful feeling" apparent in so much else is a clear revelation of the true soul, the youth and then the man.

"Death! I have met with thee—close, close at hand", a poem on the first anniversary of his escape from drowning (No. 9) is full of the real experience of clinging to life, while welcoming the sight

. . . of Him in whom my soul,
My inmost soul, delighteth . . .

and of faith in that moment of helplessness:

. . . I knew
That, though my sense was deadened, and all hope
Seemed idle, yet if I were fathoms deep
One Hand could draw me forth, and set my feet
In safety once again on Mother Earth.

So "when life was wonderfully restored to me" Frank rededicated his life to the service of God and, at eighteen, expressed in poetry his thoughts and prayers on regaining consciousness:

. . . I said:
"My gratitude must not evaporate

In idle words; I have been saved to serve!
Not only with my lips, but in my life
Must praise be given, and adoration shown."

But he continues:

. . . Oh to think that all this time
I might have been a dweller in the heavens!
That mansion in my Father's home above
Prepared for me, had not been vacant now!
And I had been with Christ, had seen His face,
The altogether lovely One . . .

And this recalled his first reactions as consciousness returned:

I dimly wondered if the gates of heaven
Had op'ed to let me in—it was not so!
The voices round me spake in earthly tones . . . it seemed as though
Those gates were closed against me evermore;
And blank dismay possessed me . . .

Meanwhile Frank was a normal natural boy. Somewhere around this time, probably while still recovering from the drowning episode, he cheerfully confessed surprise that:

Among some other lessons I am learning
While sickness lays me partly on the shelf,
I'm slowly and surprisedly discerning
What everybody knew except myself.
That even if it heard no more about me
The world would jog on easily without me.

You held a small position with some skill
And cut a fairly reasonable figure,
Then, forced to leave the place you had to fill,
You were surprised to find it wasn't bigger;
And unknown people who have watched your movements
Take up your work and do it—with improvements.

Even before he went to boarding school he set himself to lead other boys to Christ. "The Master of the Hunt" (No. 4) was written in 1910 at sixteen, when he already knew the need for perseverance,

For if you hunt the souls of men
You dare not pause for rest.

Schooldays behind him, however, and serious preparation for the service of God now occupying his mind and time, he seems to have written fewer poems—few, at least, have been preserved. One gem (No. 18):

Let HIM take all! In His employ,
His slave, I glory in my chains!

belongs to this period, 1915–17, but is undated. His physical condition had debarred him from military service, but his elder brother, Herbert, and some of his school friends had already been killed. With equal devotion Frank resolved to live or die for Christ.

MINISTER AND MISSIONARY

Frank received his theological training at the London College of Divinity (now St. John's College, Nottingham). To the delight of his friends and congregations, from then on he used the Greek New Testament as freely as if it were in English, translating colourfully as he read.

After his ordination on June 3rd, 1917, he went as curate to St. Benedict's, Liverpool, under the Rev. E. M. Benson, whose daughter married Frank's brother, Stanley. Here he met many families with menfolk at the Front. Too busy for much writing, he did record one meditation, "Songs in the Night" (No. 19) in which we can discern the spirit that sustained and carried him through the endless tribulations of his missionary and ministerial life.

O Joy in pain, in weakness Power,
Take NOW the offerings of our lips!

NOW would we own Thou hast sufficed,
Nor wait until the gloom is past—

In 1919 Frank moved with his vicar to the parish of All Saints, Preston, and was successful in leading to Christ many members of a large Bible Class for boys. A considerable number of these went into Christian service at home and abroad. One was George Scott, later Frank's colleague in West China and at Mission Headquarters in Shanghai, before joining the Staff in London and becoming Home Director in 1953. Another was Tom Isherwood, who later became Home Secretary of the Church Missionary Society. There in his digs at Preston, Frank read the life of Hudson Taylor, propping the book against his water jug during meals. Having been through it once, he started again and read the two volumes a second time. He felt that he should offer to the China Inland Mission, yet when he went to the doctor for medical approval he found that he was relieved to be told, as when he applied for military service two years previously, that he ought not to go overseas, because of the condition of his heart. The conviction that God had called him to go only deepened, however, and he realized that it was the Holy Spirit speaking to him. The wonder of being separated to the service of Christ inspired his poem, "I Trod His Earth" (No. 20):

I heard His clear, insistent Voice
Calling across the mad world's din

which ends:

Love triumphs—He shall have me.

Some months later his doctor suggested that if he had a favourable report from a specialist there might be a sporting chance of his acceptance, so on April 29th, 1920, he applied for membership of the China Inland Mission. A heart specialist approved of his acceptance for sedentary work in China; he was accepted at the Swanwick Conference and sailed for China on November 10th. His later itineraries in the hills of Szechwan completely confounded the earlier prognostication!

The impact of arrival in a pagan land and seeing godlessness undisguised—and the vulnerability of one's own Christian standards—have left few new missionaries unscathed. Only one poem records Frank Houghton's impressions, but in "Behold, I Have Told You Before" (No. 21) he cries, "It is as I feared" and

"This is the hour of Satan's power,
This is his day."

But he goes on,

IT IS AS HE SAID . . .
This is the hour of the Spirit's power . . .
Victory through the Name!

Always we find that difficulties evoked that resilient spirit in him, so that when things were at their worst and the exercise of faith most under strain, this is his message and example.

In an era of the colonial mentality, when real friendship with Chinese colleagues was sometimes regarded as unattainable, he wrote to his brother, "My heart revolts against such a theory. They are far more lovable than I expected. . . ."

The Chinese language came readily to him, and when he moved to the far western province of Szechwan, he soon adapted to the western Mandarin dialect. Fluency was necessary in the work he did, and particularly when he later returned to be Bishop. To be all things to all men had been the policy of the CIM since Hudson Taylor first led his "twenty-four willing, skilful labourers" into Inland China. But in more recent years an attitude of disillusionment and paternalism had crept into the relationships between some missionaries and the Chinese. It needed new men with open minds to bridge the gulf, and Frank was one who came to China ready to be an equal and a brother.

Life in China at that time was not easy. Following the revolution against the Manchu dynasty and the setting up of the Republic in 1912, a decade of rivalry between regional war lords had brought suffering and misery to the whole of China. Szechwan was torn and tortured by the ebb and flow of fighting and recrimination. Missionary work continued in spite of everything, foreigners sometimes enjoying a favoured status under the protection of their Governments, but often suffering with their Chinese brethren the bitterness of civilians embroiled in the conflict. Some of Frank's most moving verse was written at this time, with its resolute declaration (No. 22):

Ring'd around by Satan's power,
Ceaselessly at grips with sin,
Battle-stain'd and faint within—
"Father, save Me from this hour!"

Nay—it was for this I came! . . .

The Rt. Rev. W. W. Cassels, Bishop of West China, a member of the Cambridge Seven who so stirred Britain in 1885, recognized

Frank's godliness and ability and was glad to have him as a son-in-law when, in 1923, after a period of service in Suiting, he married Dorothy, one of the Cassels' daughters.

For Christmas, six months later, he wrote in their first home in Suiting, "Lord of Our Hearts, Immanuel" (No. 24). It was a year of banditry and warfare between rival war lords, a year of increasingly militant nationalism in which students and schoolboys shared. Always a friend of young people and popular with them, Frank had wide contacts with many in the city. Some were converted and others were very "near the Kingdom" when Frank, to whom such nationalism was a new phenomenon, urged them to have no part in the demonstrations taking place. Serious repercussions resulted, and some of his young friends were offended and left him altogether. Others followed his advice and loyally stayed with him, filled with misgivings and maligned by their contemporaries. Frank had given himself unreservedly in the spirit of "not the gospel of God only, but also our own souls" (1 Thess. 2.8) but found it all but impossible to bridge the gap between himself, the Westerner, and them, the children of millenniums of Asian culture. So he wrote (No. 24):

Thy manger-bed, how dear to us,
For there Thou camest near to us,
Lord of our hearts!

Lover of souls, we too would learn
How to come NEAR to men . . .

Nothing, O Lord, have we withheld—
Love and labour—our hearts' full store—
Still do we wait outside, repell'd,
While they but suffer us—no more! . . .

This was the year that a bandit army was given free rein to loot and rape in Suiting, so that their Mission premises were filled with refugees seeking protection, an opportunity to tell them of the love of God in Christ. It was also a year of encouragements: from units of Feng Yü-hsiang the Christian general's army, such a contrast with others; from the progress of the church girls' school in the charge of three Chinese ladies, and from some evangelistic journeys by unfrequented roads in the countryside.

During the very last sermon which Bishop Houghton preached in Canford School, he re-told the story of a boy on a riverside during one of these journeys in 1923, who was interested in a tract which Frank had given him. Because the boat on which they were travelling at the time would not wait, it was impossible to continue the conversation. The poignancy of that moment never left Frank, for the boy may never have heard the gospel again. Early one morning (perhaps with that incident in mind) as they continued their journey, the words of "I went forth to meet Him" (No. 23) came to mind and were written down. When Frank became the Editorial Secretary in London he used some of his poems from time to time, and this one was first published in *China's Millions* in 1930.

In the spring of 1924 the Houghtons moved to Paoning, the diocesan centre, and in the autumn Frank became Principal of the Theological College. Always accessible in his open home, he was in close touch with the young men who later were to be his colleagues in the Church, and gave himself to befriending them and deepening their spiritual maturity. The challenge of this strategic opportunity and the experience of being used by God to the conversion of an unsatisfactory Bible School student from another area, prompted the prayer of consecration based on Phil. 1.20, "As Always, So Now Also" (No. 25).

An epidemic broke out in the Theological College in 1925, following preaching visits by the students to the country. Frank was kept busy caring for them, but escaped infection. Bishop Cassels, however, was taken ill after visiting one gravely sick student, and Mrs. Cassels, who nursed her husband, also succumbed. Within a few days of each other both died, and the double funeral, attended by Chinese officials and acquaintances from a wide area, was used as an occasion for preaching Christ who gave His life to be "a ransom for many". Frank's sonnet, "We dare not grieve as others" (No. 26) ends, as may be expected, on the note:

While as they two pass on to their reward,
On high and lifted up, we see—the LORD.

EDITOR

Returning to England in 1926 for furlough, the Houghtons were providentially on hand when an emergency arose on the Home Staff in London. Nationalistic violence had been increasing in China, and many missionaries were being evacuated to the coast. It was inopportune for the Houghtons to go back. Then unexpectedly a new Editorial Secretary was required; if Frank accepted the appointment he would be unable to return to Szechwan. "Was it His Voice that called?" (No. 27) tells how assurance came that they should stay. So Frank was appointed and held the office for nine years. One who heard him preach at that time only remembers how his face glowed as he spoke on the words, "I believe GOD". In his first editorial in *China's Millions* he printed "As Always, So Now Also" and in April 1928 (No. 28):

He thwarted all
My fairest schemes . . .
Gave Joy above
My heart's desire.

Life in England was concerned with informing the noble army of supporters of the work in China, and calling out reinforcements for the missionaries there. The contents of *China's Millions* in those days were strong, interesting and inspiring. Personal consecration became the dominant theme in Frank's poems, and we first meet the verse which he put to music and which was used during the Centenary year of the Mission in 1965, "Let the fire burn on in my heart,

O LORD" (No. 32). He had much to do with the Comradeship for China, the children's organization of the CIM, and wrote a number of choruses, some of which are still in use.

In 1929 the General Director issued a Call to Advance, and an appeal was launched for two hundred missionaries within two years. Frank's prayer in verse, "Lord, by the call of China's need" (No. 97) was adopted and widely sung in public meetings and Mission circles until the last of the Two Hundred had sailed. So, too, the chorus "He Must Reign" (No. 34):

I want to see Thee triumphing
The whole world o'er.

But in China daunting disturbances continued. Famine and brigandage took their toll. Of three Finnish ladies who were captured by bandits, one died and the other two were killed. Mr. and Mrs. Robert Porteous and Miss Gemmel were taken but released, and two CMS missionaries were killed in Fukien. His poem entitled "When I Remember Thee" (No. 35) beginning "Trust that triumphs when fear dismays", voiced the confidence of the Mission in those dark days, when few could fail to remember that in the Boxer Rising of 1900 the toll of missionary martyrs numbered scores, and of Chinese many thousands. The Mission's leaders spoke in clear and inspiring terms, to express the steadfastness of the members, but Frank Houghton's verse summed up everything in the disarmingly simple phrases which covered all that needed to be said.

Frank's editorials in *China's Millions* and the Annual Reports could be made the subject of a worthwhile study, if this were the place for it. They also exerted a strong influence. In 1931 he wrote on the title "Warrant for Advancing", basing his thoughts on the words in Luke 4.43, "I must", and for the annual meeting he composed the hymn which has become part of the Church's treasure, "Facing a task unfinished" (No. 36). He possessed the right balance of histrionic and pietistic genius to stir the emotions with the hearts of Christians, so that their true, deep feelings of devotion to Christ and desire to glorify Him were liberated in satisfying expression, in verse and sometimes tunes which Frank created.

Before the year 1931 was out, new anxieties pressed upon the Mission and its supporters. The title of the Annual Report was *The Steep Ascent*, and "Climbing" (No. 38) was Frank's title for the poem "Landmarks along the track that lies behind", written for Freda's departure with the Two Hundred. With funds short, the Japanese threatening North China and fighting in Shanghai, and Communist militancy in Central China, "Guard the Two Hundred" (No. 98) voiced everyone's prayer.

Freda, whose curls and smiles and "tears enough to overflow the Nile" were the theme of his boyhood's phantasy, saw little service in China. After only ten months she fell ill with meningitis and went to be "with Christ, which is far better". "We do not ask Thee to explain" (No. 39) is her brother's praiseful poem which gave wings to the rejoicing sorrow of other families also.

By 1934 Frank had been working hard as Editorial Secretary for seven years and felt the need to revisit China, to renew his first-hand impressions of the place and people, and to see for himself the progress of the work. Before he left, he suffered the loss of his mother. He was away at a Swanwick Conference and Dorothy, by doctor's orders, had been consigned to bed for ten days. Stanley, who was in England at the time, was immobilized following an operation. Medical bills added to Frank's problems, but when he and Dorothy reckoned up their financial needs, after special gifts had already made it possible for her to accompany him to China, they found that they needed £20 more. Together they knelt and committed this need to the Lord—but as they rose to their feet, a knock at the door brought them a letter in the post with a cheque in it for the exact amount. This was the occasion of "My need was known to Thee alone" (No. 43). It is, incidentally, an example of almost puckish playfulness which belonged without any irreverence to some of his most serious devotional thinking—an indication of buoyant faith in his Heavenly Father.

Not long before, Mr. Ferguson, a member of the Mission, had been taken prisoner by the Communist forces and was not heard of again. Arnolis Hayman and Alfred Bosshardt had been captured and were only released in precarious health after 413 and 560 days, respectively, of suffering. Then John and Betty Stam were taken in Anhwei and beheaded. The news reached Mission Headquarters in

Shanghai while the Houghtons were there. It was a questionable time at which to begin a tour of the country.

A thought which had for long been in Frank's mind that "Though He was rich, yet for your sakes He became poor", finally took shape while he was travelling over the mountains of Szechwan, in the beautiful Christmas hymn "Thou who wast rich beyond all splendour" (No. 44).

Many long journeys had to be taken by broken-down "buses" which were little more than old lorries converted to passenger use. To find one going in the right direction on the right day was frequently a problem, and to wait patiently in uncomfortable circumstances, while roadside repairs were carried out, demanded patience and even fortitude. "Along the road His wisdom planned" (No. 46) was the product of one of these itineraries, in the company of John Sinton, then Superintendent in West Szechwan. Frank also attended several church and missionary conferences, where he was called upon to speak, and "Give me new faith in the power of Thy Name" (No. 42) was his prayer for spiritual power in service.

The Rt. Rev. John Holden was Bishop of West China, a diocese the size of England and Wales with poor communications, too extensive for effective oversight. When Frank was in Chengtu, the bishop, impressed by his qualities, asked him if he would be willing to return as bishop of a new diocese of East Szechwan. The magnitude of the task in such days as those did not escape him, and the title of his poem "God's Response—and Mine" (No. 45) says as much as the verse itself. He was willing.

Back in England, Frank was busy reporting his observations in the *Millions*, at the annual meeting, and on many other occasions, and completed his book *China Calling*. But the time to return to China soon arrived. His theme at their valedictory meeting in 1936 was "The pressure of God", and in the last issue of *China's Millions* which he edited, "The hand of the Lord was strong upon me" (Ezek. 3.14). "A Secret Joy" (No. 47) voices in a single breath his attitude as he sailed again to take up his duties as bishop.

BISHOP

On their arrival once more in China, it looked as if the Devil was desperately trying to eliminate the Houghtons, when their boat struck a rock in the Yangtze Gorges, but on St. Paul's Day, January 25th, 1937, Frank was consecrated Bishop of East Szechwan by Bishop Norris of North China, Bishop Holden of West China, and Assistant Bishops Sung and Ku, the latter a converted Muslim who was Frank's colleague for the next three years. The service, and later all synods and committees, were conducted in the Chinese language, and the Houghtons often lived and ate together with the Chinese. Frank's old students rallied round him and he gave them his love and confidence. In his reports and despatches there comes a clearly detectable development of personality and power.

For nearly four years he was engaged in almost incessant travel in his diocese. In spite of brigandage, flooded roads, scarcity of food and, latterly, bombing by the Japanese, he was able to keep all his engagements, to interview personally all his confirmation candidates, to consult at length with church leaders and Mission Councils, and to deal with the correspondence and problems left in the wake of the Communist Long March. The simplicity of "Whither He Sends" (No. 48) reflects the unburdened simplicity of Frank's faith in Him who said, "Lo, I am with you always". Following a conference of missionaries in Chühsien, one wrote, "Many of us could testify that the Lord 'showed Himself again to His disciples'." This theme Frank expressed in the poem "Reveal Thyself Again" (No. 49), and his lines,

The day is dawning on our weariness,
Our long night's labour and our ill-success

tell in the imagery of the Galilean fishermen the experience of himself and his colleagues.

In East Szechwan there were no railways and few roads. Some rivers were navigable to wooden junks, laboriously dragged upstream by teams of toiling "trackers", but elsewhere, over the hilly and mountainous hinterland, all travel had to be by foot or *huakan*, a makeshift sedan chair like a deckchair slung between two poles. The great compensation of such slow progress was time for thought and even for reading, John Wesley-like. In wartime Bishop Houghton travelled 1,300 miles through his province of seventeen counties in these ways. To this period we owe his "Hymn of Praise to Jesus Enthroned" (No. 50) beginning,

Down in the darkest depths of shame
My sinless Lord was found

and the Christmas carol, "The thronging angels hailed His birth" (No. 52) which was probably written in 1939.

Another hymn, printed in Shanghai on a greetings card after Frank became General Director, was "The Heart's Journey" (No. 53):

O Thou who dost direct my feet

again inspired by "journeyings oft". "The hymn," he explained to a friend in 1967, "came to me when I was reading 2 Thessalonians in my Greek Testament as I travelled . . . I was impressed by the fact that the [Greek] word 'guide' occurs only three times in the New Testament, Luke 1.79, 1 Thess. 3.11 and then 2 Thess. 3.5, where the journey is not a physical but a spiritual one. The same God who directs our steps (as He guided my travels over hill and dale in Szechwan) also guides our hearts. How often I have prayed that He will direct my heart *into His love,* into the *depths* of that love, until not only is my heart *warmed* thereby but, as a result, I respond and begin to love as He loves! . . . I want my heart to be directed into that steadfastness which Christ showed when He *set His face* to go to Jerusalem—to the Cross."

"He loved his home and a quiet settled life," Mrs. Houghton wrote in a further comment on this hymn. "But at this time he was travelling round, though he was never strong. . . . Travel was his lot in life—though this was only one aspect of his steadfast endurance under all circumstances."

From December 1938 to January 1939, the Mission Council, composed of all Directors and Superintendents and others, met in Shanghai to "seek the Lord's face" and thrash out Mission policy. An uneasy peace in Europe had been secured at Munich. China and Japan had been at war for almost two years already, and the Japanese had taken all the long coast of China and its ports, including Hankow and Canton. Frank Houghton was asked to write the official Council report "The Pattern Shown".

Mr. George Gibb, General Director in succession to D. E. Hoste, another of the Cambridge Seven, was already elderly and failing in health. During the next few months, Frank was frequently asked to allow his name to go forward for election as the next General Director. Meanwhile, war broke out in Europe and the repercussions on Missions in China were clearly predictable. Without mention of his personal predicament, his agony, the agony of many who knew what war entailed, led him late in 1939 to affirm his faith in the tense poem, "If in this strange eventful year—" (No. 51). It needed "our desperate case" to "prove Thee, Lord".

So Frank's eyes were wide open when, on December 1st, he wrote to Dorothy from a Chinese wayside inn somewhere on his travels in the diocese, that he had written to Mr. Gibb, saying that he could not definitely refuse to be nominated. Only a most courageous man, with tremendous faith in God, could have consented to undertake the leadership of an international Mission of over a thousand members in a country at war and with more than one German Associate Mission under his direction and care, when Germany was at war with Britain. But his faith was equal to it. On February 1st, 1940, he wrote in his diary, also in an inn,

When place we seek (I have not done that!)
Or place we shun (Is there a danger of my doing this?)
The soul finds happiness in none.
But with my God to point the way
'Tis equal joy to go or stay. (Have I reached the point where I can really regard it as equal joy to stay in Szechwan or go to Shanghai?)

GENERAL DIRECTOR

Inexorably the wheels turned. On April 15th, 1940, Mr. Gibb, the retiring General Director, nominated Frank to be his successor and the approval of all Mission Councils and senior members was awaited. Then, from his bed only two or three weeks before he died, in the presence of three Directors and the China Secretary, Mr. Gibb made the formal appointment on October 21st, 1940.

With the pressure of responsibility and work heavily upon him, the new General Director might understandably have found little time or freedom in which to compose more verse. But it was his nature to give expression in poetry to his soul's deepest meditations. Like trout rising to a fly, it breaks the surface of his life's deep waters, and the ripples spread and go on spreading. One such is the prayer (No. 56):

From Thee is all my expectation, Lord,
O speak the word—
Thy servant waits for Thee.

The story is well known of Hudson Taylor quietly whistling the tune of "Jesus, I am resting, resting" when news of serious rioting and danger to missionaries was received in 1877. The chuckle is detectable in Frank Houghton's poem, "I Have a Wealthy Father" (No. 57), which is his reaction to the tightening grip of economic stringencies and delayed mails. War was absorbing the interest and concern of more and more supporters of the Mission, as they became involved or their assets were immobilized. His spirit soon infected his fellow missionaries, and the warmth of fellowship and harmony spread through their ranks.

But they were increasingly difficult years upon which the Mission under his leadership was launched. A sequence of titles exposes the tensions, the deprivations and fears, as the war intensified.

Bishop and Mrs. Houghton were in North America on Mission business in 1941 when Japan struck at Pearl Harbour and pulverized the Pacific fleet of the United States. Soon the whole East Asian area was being overrun by the Japanese. With prophetic insight, Emergency Headquarters for the CIM had already been set up in Chungking, but before long sixty members of the Mission were interned as enemy aliens in Shanghai, sixty more at Temple Hill and then Weihsien with about one hundred children of the Chefoo Schools, and forty more missionaries in other Japanese-occupied areas.

For Bishop and Mrs. Houghton to return to China via the Pacific was impossible; Europe, in spite of war, was the only hope and there was business to be conducted there also. The Atlantic was crossed without mishap and Frank spoke at the annual meeting in London in 1942. But civilian travel in wartime was difficult to arrange, even for a bishop with responsibility for a thousand men, women and children in a theatre of war. In November 1942 Frank and Dorothy started out for Chungking via South Africa, hindered by storms and U-boats. After four months they had progressed only as far as South Africa. There Frank negotiated with the Government for a fruit farm in Natal to be made available if the interned children of the Chefoo Schools could be released through the mediation of the International Red Cross. The exchange never took place. The Houghtons' ship was torpedoed while they were ashore, but by the first one available they continued their journey to Ceylon and India and from there by air to Chungking. Through all the difficulties and dangers of these days, the words rang in Frank's heart:

Eternal Love enfolds them every one
Who trust in Thee, through Jesus Christ Thy Son.

Access to Free China had at first become limited to dangerous routes through the mountains from Burma, and finally by air from

India over Japanese-occupied territory. Some mail even came through Tibet, yet Frank's light-hearted confidence in his Heavenly Father is revealed in poems such as, "Though Every Road Were Barred" (No. 58).

With John Sinton, whom he had appointed Deputy China Director, Frank Houghton bore the burden, the stringency and the great emotional stresses of leadership until world peace was restored. No wonder sleep began to evade him. Singapore had fallen to the Japanese and it was all but impossible for anyone to move within the areas under their control. Nevertheless, the Rev. Marcus Cheng, a much respected Bible teacher, succeeded in escaping from Singapore and making his way through enemy territory all the way to Free China. His unexpected arrival in Chungking was the answer to the prayers and resolutions of a conference of missionaries held in Kansu under the General Director's leadership, at which the establishment of a training institution for Chinese church leaders of the future was given high priority. Young Chinese men and women were waiting to avail themselves of the teaching. Before long the Chungking Theological Seminary had been set up with Marcus Cheng at its head.

Among his missionaries were some preparing to set out on new pioneering ventures after Frank's own heart. Words he had written in his book, *China Calling,* had been the means God used to call into being one such venture among a million unevangelized Nosu people in the Taliangshan. Encouraged by these evidences of the hand of God at work, Frank wrote a letter to the Mission and a poem under the familiar title "God is Working His Purpose out" (No. 60):

Spirit of God, Thou hast Thy men
Waiting Thy time to do Thy will.

During those days in 1942–43, funds were very low and the exchange rate in China was disadvantageous. Wartime rationing provided for Chungking residents only, but streams of missionaries were passing through and had to be fed. One day, when there was no bread and the flour supply was finished, a telephone message was received from the hospital across the river. Would some flour be useful? They had some extra bags. "What shall I do when the brook runs dry?" (No. 61) is faith's testimony in such a situation. Every mealtime was an occasion for praise and for prayer during those difficult days. "By Thy command our table has been spread" (No. 62) was one of Frank's "graces" frequently used; and another:

Thy gracious provision has spread us this board
Help us to eat to Thy glory, O Lord.

Who in those days could forget the "G.D.'s" relaxed, smiling, friendly way with every member of the Mission, or fail to enjoy his infectious laughter? "Whose laughing shoulders ever pumped up and down as delightfully as Frank Houghton's?"

The long nightmare of war was coming to an end. With a marvelling backward glance, all eyes were looking forward to peace and liberty of movement restored. Since Hudson Taylor took "Ebenezer" and "Jehovah Jireh" ("Hitherto hath the Lord helped us—The Lord will provide") as a watchword of the China Inland Mission, God's faithfulness in the past had been strong ground for dependence on His undertaking in the future. So, with his New Year message for 1945, Frank gave the Mission his twin verses, "How plain and clear the steps appear" and "Since Thy Hand my day has planned" (No. 64).

"We have never known such opportunities," the General Director wrote when the Pacific as well as the European war had ended, Mission Headquarters had returned to Shanghai and the long occupied areas of China became accessible again. There were churches and suffering Christians to be visited, comforted and encouraged in the resumption of their witness. There were endless possibilities for advance in the north-west and south-west, in the universities and in new spheres of Christian literature and radio broadcasting. Following the success of the pioneering phase of missionary work, the great new factor, "The Chinese Church", faced Missions.

Back in 1943 the China Council, planning for the future, laid emphasis on the leadership of the Church in China being in Chinese hands, and foreign missionaries working "through the Chinese Church". This had been the Founder's policy long years before, but in the changing climates of Western political dominance and China's post-Revolution chaos, strong missionary initiative had become the entrenched pattern. As General Director, Frank Houghton's vision and leadership were nowhere more far-seeing than in this new emphasis. He saw the Mission as an active body of hard-working friends of the Church, without officiousness or interference, helping it to set up and furnish its own house in the post-war years.

"Our aim," he wrote, "is to assist in building up the Church throughout the land" . . . "the Mission engages in pioneer evangelism where no church exists, with a view to establishing new churches which in turn will spread the light. China will never be evangelized except by the Thessalonian method 'from *you* sounded out the word of the Lord' ". Arnold Lea, who later became Assistant General Director, wrote after Frank Houghton's death, "Frank's vision for the Church when he became General Director has really formed the present policies of the Mission." It inspired Arnold Lea's own axiom "A church in every community and THEREBY the gospel to every creature!" Although in some ways it reiterated Hudson Taylor's strategy, in other ways Bishop Houghton's lead anticipated emphases which at the time were not generally adopted, as now, throughout the Christian world.

Frank's leading articles at this time bore titles like "God's Triumph" and "Attack". He did not write his verse with a view to publication. Often his poems lay fallow for years before others were permitted to share them. But when he was "everyone's Bishop", with thousands of Chinese and missionaries as his colleagues, he increasingly shared his poetry and his happy jingles with them. Early verse was quoted again and new expressions of joy and faith appeared in *China's Millions* and the *Field Bulletin*. "When I think of my Father's eternal design" (No. 65) may not be textbook poetry, but, as the spontaneous overflow of a child of God rejoicing in his Father's goodness, it is pure Frank Houghton.

One of his first post-war journeys was to Germany and Scandinavia to renew fellowship with the Associate Missions—not that spiritual fellowship had been broken, for German missionaries had done all they could to help members of the Mission interned by the Japanese, and Germans in Free China had worked and prayed in unbroken unity with Allied missionaries.

"Just before midnight on June 13th, 1948," Frank wrote on his card of greetings for 1949, "I was in a train at Marburg, Germany, about to leave for the north, after a delightful conference with Associate workers of the CIM. On the station platform stood many of the leaders of the great Deaconess Fellowship. . . . While the train delayed they sang the hymn by Cornelius Krummacher (1824–84) of which this is a poor translation. The melody haunted me all through the night, and later when I discovered the beauty of the conception behind the words, I felt that the hymn ought to be sung in English. Part of the succinctness of the original has been sacrificed to rhyme and rhythm in the translation. . . ." So "Star whose light shines o'er me" (No. 66) has joined the treasury in our English hymn-books. Another hymn translated from the German by W. H. Wilhelm and Frank Houghton together, is "Lord Jesus Christ, the work is Thine" (No. 67).

Throughout the war the Communists had been secure in their Yenan quarters in north Shensi, reserving their strength for action when the Japanese defeat was won. Few believed that they possessed the potential, not only to seize Manchuria and the northern provinces, but to overrun the whole of China. As their success proceeded and the menace to the Church increasingly became apparent, hearts sank. "Have we not been through enough? Are we not now to have peace to consolidate our work and advance?" many were thinking. But in four brief years their hopes were dashed. "Knowing Thee, I cannot doubt" and "When God is silent for a space" (Nos. 69, 70) reflect the growing concern of the leaders whose hopes had been set so high. To the *Millions* Frank Houghton now contributed an article entitled "Crisis" in which he said, "In view of what GOD has begun to do . . . should we not be failing Him miserably if we were to be infected by the climate of opinion around us, and merely waited for a Communist triumph? Therefore we are not planning for evacuation. . . . Our present purpose is to hold on."

New missionaries were allowed to proceed to China and some of our senior stalwarts of today were amongst them. However, by May 1949 Shanghai had fallen to the Communists and by the end of the year they were in control of even the remotest west. Even so, the Communist strategy was initially a gloved-hand approach and although work was all but halted, religious liberty was perfidiously proclaimed in giant letters on city walls. Late in 1950, although at times suffering severely from insomnia, Bishop Houghton could write triumphantly, "We hold on throughout China, watching events—but not as mere observers, since by believing prayer we are participating in God's purposes."

Finally, after his own state of health had compelled him to commit the administration of the Mission to his fellow directors for a few months while he recuperated in Australia, the situation in China deteriorated and the very presence of foreigners imperilled Chinese Christians. A general withdrawal became imperative and Frank Houghton issued what was, as he called it, the most important statement he had ever made: "Co-operation with the Chinese Church has ceased to be possible ... the majority of CIM missionaries must plan to withdraw."

He called a Conference of Mission Directors at Kalorama, near Melbourne, and in an atmosphere of unanimous conviction that the end of the Mission's current service in China did not mean the end of its existence but a re-commissioning to other East Asian countries, a call to re-form and advance was issued to all the homelands. What could have been the death knell of the Mission became the rallying call that eventually launched the Overseas Missionary Fellowship on its way. At a time when many were saying, "You're finished! Admit it!" this cable came from the Directors' Conference:

> LENGTHEN CORDS! STRENGTHEN STAKES!
> WHILE EMPHASIZING PRIORITY PRAYER FOR CHINA
> CONFERENCE UNANIMOUSLY CONVINCED MISSION SHOULD
> EXPLORE UNMET NEED PREPARATORY TO ENTERING NEW
> FIELDS FROM THAILAND TO JAPAN. HAGGAI 2.5.
> ("My Spirit abides among you; fear not".)

Conferences of missionaries were held in Hong Kong, where many recently out of China were still congregated, and in the main Mission centres. Some could not see that a closely knit, battle-hardened unit of hundreds of experienced evangelists, Bible teachers, and medical men and women who had hitherto worked in only one country could make a significant contribution to the evangelization of neglected populations of South-east Asia, Japan and Taiwan. But the conferences as a whole gave strong support to the Kalorama declaration.

In November 1951 twenty-five Directors, leaders and elected representatives of the rank and file met in England at Bournemouth. Frank well knew the tensions that existed, and that some questioned the rightness of his continuing to lead the Mission, after all that he had done and suffered in the last twelve and a half eventful years. Giving, as always, a clear spiritual tone to the Conference, he began by making the whole issue of liquidation or continuance of the Mission and his own part in it open to discussion. Step by step a new pattern for the future was given, as the Conference waited upon God. Survey teams had already been despatched to several East Asian countries, and their reports indicated both the immensity of the needs and opportunities and the difficulties and dangers, not least from Communist insurgence. Communist terrorists had a stranglehold on Malaya; the French had their backs to the wall in Indo-China; the Hukbalahaps were at the gates of Manila, and the prospects were dark and grim. But the command of God was plainly to re-form and attack again.

Frank knew that he could not keep going indefinitely, but his spirit rose to the challenge of new frontiers and to have a part in claiming them for Christ would have been pure joy to him. Under his chairmanship, the Conference determined to advance on these new fronts as the "China Inland Mission OVERSEAS MISSIONARY FELLOWSHIP", with the principles and message of the Mission unchanged. Then, with agonizing heart-searching and tears in which every strong man around the Conference table shared, there came the realization that Frank Houghton, who had borne so many years of crisis and heartbreak, could not be asked to continue as leader in the new era, when the resilience and adaptability of a younger man would be essential. Frank's serenity when this shattering decision was reached was impressive. He was faint, perplexed and no doubt heartbroken, but trusting and even radiant in his acceptance of the will of God, having insisted before discussion began that he was ready to continue or to stand down. He continued as Consulting Director while younger men led the new advance into the unknown future of the Mission.

Small wonder, then, that when he found himself out of active missionary service a pall of dismay descended upon him. In an article which he wrote for *The Millions,* he told of two visions which the Lord in His gracious love gave him at this time, to strengthen his resilience. In the first, "It seemed as if I was going into thick darkness, and I was alone. But the picture scarcely formed itself in my mind when it was as if a strong Hand clasped mine and I heard a Voice that said, 'Did you not know that I should be here?' Then I knew that this was 'the thick darkness *where God was*' (Exod. 20.21)." So his greetings card for 1952 carried his poem "The Thick Darkness": "I thought I was walking all alone" (No. 71).

Again at the close of the year, he had a vision "of Christ going forth conquering and to conquer, and I saw that He was moving forward with such certainty and such joy that my pain and sufferings seemed utterly unimportant to me. . . . All my circumstances, my trials, my temptations, were as entanglements out of which I sprang to my feet unencumbered and followed Him. . . . What do they matter as long as God is exalted? . . ."

THE LAST TWENTY YEARS

New horizons of service now opened for Bishop Houghton, but in a pastoral setting very different from what he had just left. During 1952 he wrote *If We Believe* for the Inter-Varsity Fellowship, re-issued in 1961 under the title *Faith's Unclaimed Inheritance*, and in 1953 his powerful biography of Amy Carmichael of Dohnavur was published. In February 1952, he became the vicar of St. Mark's, Leamington Spa, and that year his Christmas card carried the text, "O taste and see how gracious the Lord is; blessed is the man that trusteth in him", with the poem beginning "We taste and we are satisfied" (No. 72).

After a year or two in the parish of St. Mark's, meeting problems and discouragements of many kinds, "The Answer of God" came for his own comfort and the encouragement of many others (No. 73):

As bright hopes faded, stair by stair
Down plunged the prophet to despair.

Here again, the powerful feeling of his own experiences comes through in an unmuted honesty of self-revelation.

By the end of 1955 some of the problems had been alleviated. Land was procured and a vicarage built; in answer to prayer over £5,000 were supplied to cover expenses. "Hallow this house, O Lord, we pray" (No. 74) was the dedication hymn sung outside the new vicarage before their friends were invited in to see what God had given for the church.

But with the parish growing rapidly and his many activities proving too much, a change to lighter responsibilities became advisable. For eight years from 1955 to 1963 he had written "Daily Bread" notes for the Scripture Union and served as a Vice-President of the Inter-Varsity Fellowship of Evangelical Unions and President of the Chinese Overseas Christian Mission, as well as preaching and taking confirmation services in many parts of the country. He was now sixty-four and, following his doctor's advice, began to pray for a quieter living; but the answer did not come at once, and "Waiting, if He bids me wait" (No. 77) is the willing servant's soliloquy.

Then the living of St. Peter's, Drayton, near Banbury in Oxfordshire, was offered to him, a parish with a small church which had had no rector for a whole year. In *The Problem of Pain* C. S. Lewis says, "Our Father refreshes us on the journey with some pleasant inns, but will not encourage us to mistake them for home." Drayton had a large rectory and garden, and from 1960 to 1963 this was the Houghtons' "pleasant inn". "My Father has a rest-house" (No. 78), which echoes C. S. Lewis's theme, and (No. 79),

My Lord, who in the desert fed
On soul-sustaining heavenly Bread,

composed in 1961 for the 350th anniversary of the Authorized Version of the Bible, are the sweet fruits of that haven. The same year, attempts were made to bring legislation before Parliament which would have undermined Sunday as a day of rest, the Lord's Day. Bishop Houghton wrote a memorandum addressed to the Departmental Committee of the Home Office, and letters to the press and to Members of Parliament on the subject. "A Psalm or Song for the Lord's Day" (No. 80) was written and sung at Drayton and sent to friends for Christmas 1962.

In 1963, now sixty-nine years of age, Frank Houghton retired, but, praying about where they were to go, was led to Parkstone, Poole, where the vicar had no curate and needed help. "If I had left the pathway of Thy will" (No. 81) is a meditation on Exod. 23.20, "Behold, I send an Angel before thee, to keep thee in the way, and to bring thee into the place which I have prepared", and Gen. 24.27, "I being in the way, the Lord led me". For the past ten and a half years he had carried the duties of his own parishes; even in retirement he was active in the ministry until his last illness.

Preparations were in hand to celebrate the Centenary of the China Inland Mission, and Frank was asked to prepare a book to mark the occasion. He chose to edit an anthology of prose and verse under the forward-looking title *The Fire Burns On*, and contributed to it several of his own earlier poems and a new Centennial hymn (No. 84). Predictably, it looks backward only to look far ahead; back to the work in China but focusing on the living, suffering Church of today, and forward "along new trails" to "let Thy Name be glorified" and "to bring Thy kingdom in".

In time the lease of their convenient flat in Poole expired. Where should they move next? What did the future hold? There is a poignancy in the simple verse, "Dark and dim is the road ahead" (No. 85) and another (No. 86):

Conscious of weakness, I may claim
STRENGTH that is promised in Thy Name.

Another flat was offered to them close to the church and shops, which came as a great relief. Mrs. Houghton had been critically ill and events in the world outside were deeply distressing, yet Frank Houghton wrote, "Let the world's turmoil still increase—in Thee, my Saviour, there is *peace*".

At seventy-five, in 1969, "The Challenge" (No. 87) is as virile as anything he wrote in his prime:

Should doors be barred—in simple trust
Alert we wait the trumpet call

and his Christmas card for 1970 read "Certain hope for the New Year", "The Lord God Omnipotent reigneth (Rev. 19.6). Thanks be to God!" During the year he preached a series of sermons on 1 Cor. 13.13, "Now abideth faith, hope, love, these three; but the greatest of these is love", and once again he drew upon his verse of 1933, "Give me new faith in the power of Thy Name" (No. 42).

Christmas 1971 was marked by a card which conjures up afresh the gallantry of this Faithful, as he nears the end of his pilgrim way:

"They go from strength to strength" (Ps. 84.7)

That, having all things done
And all your conflicts past,
Ye may o'ercome through Christ alone
And stand complete at last.

With the New Year, Moses' words in Exodus 33.18 were in his mind when he wrote (No. 88):

Show me Thy glory, Lord,
To the year's end.

But he could almost have used the words, "To my life's end", for during the year his health failed and he was taken into Cornford House, the Mission's home for retired members. There, on the thirty-fifth anniversary of his consecration as Bishop, January 25th, 1972, Frank Houghton heard the call to meet Him whom he so loved and to be with Him for ever. The words of the apostle Paul, "For me to live is Christ and to die is gain", were true also for Frank, and the prayer of the Lord Jesus,

"I will that they whom Thou hast given me
be with me where I am, that they may behold
my glory" (John 17.24)

was triumphantly fulfilled for His faithful servant.

SCHOOLDAYS

The best homage we can give Him is to live gladly and merrily for His love.
Lady Julian of Norwich

—words which greatly influenced Frank Houghton's life.

1 THE NIGHT IS DARK

The night is dark, and over all the world,
The banner of the foe has been unfurled.
  The fight is fierce and long—
  The foe is strong.

But in the eastern sky the morning breaks,
A morning without clouds, the morn awakes.
  The night has passed away,
  And comes the day.

The Sun of Righteousness Himself appears,
Dispels the gloom, and drives away our fears;
  In all His power He reigns,
  And peace maintains.

December 27th, 1908

The night is dark

Frank wrote this poem when he was fourteen, after hearing a sermon on Luke 1.78, 79: ". . . the dayspring from on high hath visited us, To give light to them that sit in darkness and in the shadow of death, to guide our feet into the way of peace".

2 A CHRISTMAS CAROL

1. Loud songs of exultation raise,
   To greet the new-born King;
We lift our voices in Thy praise,
   With thankful hearts we sing:
      Rejoice and praise the Lord our God,
         That on this happy morn,
      To save His people from their sin,
         The Lord is born!

2. The mighty God has come to earth,
   His wondrous power hath shown;
Now let the tidings of His birth
   O'er all the world be known.
      Rejoice and praise, etc.

3. He is the everlasting Lord,
   The glorious Prince of Peace.
His presence brightens every heart,
   And makes all sorrows cease.
      Rejoice and praise, etc.

December 1908

Loud songs of exultation raise

A Christmas Carol from the Beaufort Hymnal, the family manuscript hymnal compiled by E. M. and A. T. Houghton in 1910. It is set to the tune *Gaudete* (No. 113 in the Church Hymnal.)

3 I AM THINE

I am Thine, O my Saviour, for Thou hast redeemed me,
And blotted my sins like a cloud from Thy sight;
Or ever the earth and the heavens were fashioned,
Thou madest me Thine, in Thy love and Thy might.

I am Thine, O my Saviour; in perfect submission
I bow to Thy will—it is ever the best:
We see but the present, our God sees the future,
And leaning on Him we may peacefully rest.

I am Thine, O my Saviour; my love is but feeble,
And oft-times I fall when temptations assail;
But Thou art the same, and Thy love is unbounded,
Thou grantest me pardon whenever I fail.

I am Thine, O my Saviour; the waves may be mighty
That burst o'er the rocks and ascend to the sky,
But fear will depart, for my Saviour is with me,
In the midst of the tempest He whispers, " 'Tis I!"

April 8th, 1909

I am Thine, O my Saviour

A note in Frank's handwriting runs: "Poem written April 8th, 1909, the first anniversary of my confirmation". He often spoke of having such joy on that occasion that, "As I walked the mile from the church to my home, I was saying to my Saviour over and over again, 'Lord, I am Thine!' "

When you are weary in the chase
  Because the way is long,
When there's a slackening in the pace,
  A dullness in the song—
Look up into the Master's Face,
  Take courage, and be strong!

For when it seems the chance is lost,
  And all your ardour dies,
When others bid you count the cost,
  And urge you to be "wise",
Then mark how bright still gleams the light
  Deep in the Master's eyes!

For if you hunt the souls of men
  You dare not pause for rest;
At every fall you rise again,
  Though baffled and distressed,
You cannot doubt the issue when
  The Master rides abreast!

1910

When you are weary

Though published under the date May 22nd, 1918, in *The Clarencian*, the magazine of Clarence School, now Canford School in Dorset, Frank wrote it when he was sixteen. In 1928 as Editor of *China's Millions* he made use of it again in an article on "Looking Back" (Luke 9.62), "for those who look up to Him never look back".

"While I was at boarding school," he wrote, "the desire to witness for Christ and to introduce Him to my friends grew stronger and stronger. I began to keep a list of boys for whom I prayed daily." That list was never laid aside but grew as the years passed. Frank's "boys" and their children had a special place in his heart. In later years those "greatly loved", for whom he prayed regularly, numbered over eighty. (See also Introduction, page 17.)

5 THE DEATH OF CHRIST

O Thou of men rejected and despised,
Who yet despised the shame of all Thy woes,
Who suffered on the cross, and then uprose,
Who gave up life, by men so highly prized,
To bear the guilt that we should else have borne—
Be near, we pray Thee, while we meditate
On Thine amazing love, and on the hate
That crowned Thee with that cruel crown of thorn
        And nailed Thee on the tree—
For, oh! Thy death has given new life to me!

For Thou wast holy, harmless, undefiled,
And not a stain of guilt in Thee was found,
Nor didst Thou speak to those who pressed around,
One angry word, though beaten and reviled.
Words are too weak Thine anguish to express;
And we, poor sinful mortals, we who fell
In our first father's fall, can never tell
The weight—the burden—of our guiltiness.
        They nailed Thee on the tree—
And yet Thy death has given new life to me!

continued

Thou, Lord, wast crucified for us, that we,
Who cannot save ourselves, might yet be saved,
That, though by nature sinful and depraved,
Our hearts might yet be washed and cleansed by Thee.
Thou art Almighty—and the soldiers' spears
Could nothing have availed against Thy Hand,
If Thou hadst willed their fury to withstand,
But Love in all Thine earthly life appears.
    The sacrifice was free—
And, Lord, Thy death has given new life to me!

April 9th and 10th, 1911

O Thou of men rejected

This poem bore the dedication "To Alfred Houghton, who this day, April 11th, 1911, has attained the age of fifteen years, the following short poem is dedicated". "He is despised and rejected of men", Isa. 53.3. "Who . . . endured the cross, despising the shame", Heb. 12.2.

6 THOUGH EMPIRES FALL

Though empires fall and kingdoms may decay,
And though they rot before our very sight,
In all their majesty, and power, and might,
Thy Word, O God, shall never pass away!
As year succeeds to year, and day to day,
To those whose souls are wrapp'd in darkest night,
Still doth the entrance of Thy Word give light,
And in it still they find support and stay.
The secret of the greatness of our land,
The Book that tames the wild and savage breast,
And carries peace and freedom in its hand,
By which the souls of thousands have been blest—
Let men deride it, and its truth withstand!
On Thee and on Thy Word, secure we rest!

March 20th, 1911

Though empires fall

"A Sonnet on the Tercentenary of the Authorized Version of the Bible". Printed in the *Bath Chronicle*. Fifty years later Frank was to write the hymn, "My Lord, who in the desert fed" for the 350th anniversary.

7 CORONATION HYMN

Lord Almighty, Thou who reignest
  In the heavens for evermore,
Thou who, e'en on earth, ordainest
  Who shall reign on every shore:
Thou art He who, crowned with glory,
  Hast made all Thy foes to flee;
Mightiest monarchs quail before Thee,
  At Thy feet they bow the knee.

Lord, we come to Thee, confessing
  Power and glory both are Thine;
And we pray Thee that Thy blessing
  On our monarch's head may shine.
Though o'er countless millions reigning,
  May he own Thy gracious name;
Rev'rent fear of Thee retaining,
  Though he win all earthly fame.

Grant him grace to battle ever
  On the side of truth and right;
And, through weakness, may he never
  Bend the knee to Satan's might.
Lord, temptations may assail him,
  That we cannot feel or know;
May Thy Spirit never fail him,
  May he vanquish every foe.

continued

May he be our Faith's Defender,
  To his oaths may he be true;
Ever pitiful and tender
  To the poor, whose joys are few.
Bless our Queen in fullest measure,
  And, when dawns that last great day,
May they both receive that treasure
  Which can never fade away!

1911

Lord Almighty, Thou who reignest

This is a hymn written "on the occasion of the Coronation of their Majesties King George V and Queen Mary"; printed on sheets headed "Kensington Episcopal Chapel, Bath" and set to the tune *Austria*, with the author's name and the address 2 Beaufort East, Bath. Frank prayed regularly for the Royal Family and more than once wrote on special occasions to express his loyal concern for their welfare.

8 THE FUTURE

Once I had said, "Oh, that I could know
  The future, and the part I have to play,
  And all the joys and sorrows of the way
That lies ahead; that Thou, O Lord, wouldst show
If all the hopes that now within me glow,
  Those hopes of pow'r and greatness that hold sway
  Within my breast, will on some far-off day
Be gratified, e'en here on earth below!"
But now I thank Thee that Thou dost not take
  That veil away, stretched out the path to hide;
I would be nothing—all things—for Thy sake
  Since Thou for me that cruel death hast died.
And when in Thine own likeness I awake,
  Then, then, O Lord, shall I be satisfied!

1912

Once I had said

This spiritually mature prayer of dedication was written seven months after Frank's escape from drowning and shortly before his eighteenth birthday. It was printed in the *Record* on March 29th, 1912. (Intro., page 15.)

9 COMMEMORATION DAY

—*"being a poem written twelve months after a narrow escape from drowning on Boscombe Beach, Friday, August 25th, 1911." (See Introduction, page 15.)*

Death! I have met with thee—close, close at hand,
When life and youth, and hopes and joys of earth
Had left no vacant space for thoughts of thee,
And of thy near approach, within my mind.
I felt thy touch, and saw thee face to face.
Aye, and thy grasp had held me with a clutch
I could not loosen, but another Hand
Stronger than mine or thine, released me, while
One to whom all must yield obedience
Said "Loose thy hold!" And straight thy gloomy visage
Retreated, and thyself confess'd defeat.
As when some traveller on the moorland lone
With careless step advances, knowing yet
That somewhere, right athwart the way, there lies
A deep, deep chasm, (where he cannot tell,
And recks but little, while the sunshine-rays
Illumine all the path), then suddenly
The sunlight fades, and all is dark and dim,
While scarce a foot divides him from the verge
Of that most dread abyss, whose darkest depths
No eye can pierce, all startled and amazed,
He seeks to turn his steps, but giddiness
Seizes his brain, sense fails, his body sways,
When lo! a friend, whose anxious eye has marked
The traveller's danger, puts a strong hand forth,
And draws him back!—So, thoughtlessly intent
On pleasure's paths, I was brought near to death,
Gaunt-visaged death, a year ago today.

continued

Deep waters closed above my head; I thought
That I had looked my last on earth and sky,
And all on earth who love me, that my eyes
Would open next on heaven, there to meet
The loving gaze of Him in whom my soul,
My inmost soul, delighteth, yet an instinct
Told me to strive for life, which few men yield
Without a struggle, so I battled on
Against the strong, deep waters helplessly.
Hope, this life's hope, died fast within me now,
And yet the time seemed long till consciousness
Departed, and the waves' wild gurgling ceas'd.
Ere this, the billow's voice was loud, unruly,
While a deep undertone roared in mine ears
Down, down beneath the surface. Calm at last
Was mine, untroubled calm, and then—a blank.
And yet I live, I move, I speak my thoughts,
And those I love are near me; what remains
To tell me that my mortal pilgrimage,
My life on earth, was perilously near
Its ending, but a year ago today?

And now I thank Thee, Lord, that in that hour,
Although my mind was dull, and thought inactive,
Ere yet the wearying struggle in my brain
Had given place to calm unconsciousness,
And suffocation's work was ended, then
Out of the depths I cried to Thee, my God!
'Twas but the cry of Peter, when he sank,
As I, beneath the treacherous ocean-waves—
The wind grew boisterous, faith and courage failed,
And o'er the billows came that cry of fear
To One whose ears are open, "Help me, Lord!"
The untaught fisherman of Galilee
Knew that in One, One only, was his hope,
And if He failed—such thought is blasphemy!

continued

Is His arm shortened that it cannot save?
Is His ear heavy that He cannot hear
His people's faltering cry? Thou heardest me!
For Thou hast said to all that fear Thy Name
Thou wilt be with them—though the waters roar,
The floods shall not o'erflow them; and I knew
That, though my sense was deadened, and all hope
Seemed idle, yet, if I were fathoms deep,
One Hand could draw me forth, and set my feet
In safety once again on Mother Earth.

The heathen poet, Horace, when a tree
Had all but crushed him, in no comic vein
Tells us that, like a shipwrecked mariner
He has hung up his garments, all sea-drenched
To great Oceanus, the sailors' god.
Did Faunus turn aside the falling trunk?
To Faunus will he sacrifice a lamb,
Such offering as his means permit; and I,
When life was wondrously restored to me,
I offered up my sacrifice of praise
To Him who is, and was, and is to come.
Thoughts crowded in upon me; and I said:
"My gratitude must not evaporate
In idle words; I have been saved to serve!
Not only with my lips, but in my life
Must praise be given, and adoration shown.
Perchance Death's prey escaped him, that my Lord
Might use me in His service; may I then
Be as a chosen vessel in His sight,
Meet for my Master's use, to bear His Name
Before the world around me! May the lamp
That burns but dimly now within my soul
Be as a shining light reflecting Thee,
Light of the World!" . . . But restless Time passed on.

continued

A year has glided silently away,
That solemn warning has been half-forgot.
My life has changed but little. Still the world,
The flesh, and Satan, strive within my breast
To oust all thoughts of Him. Now, as I pause,
And think again of my deliverance
A year ago today, may grace be given
To baffle all temptation, that henceforth
In soul and body I may glorify
The Lord whose mercy was vouchsafed to me,
Unworthy of all favour. May these words
Be no mere platitudes, no empty phrases,
But the deep aspirations of a heart
Surrendered wholly to its Master's will!
Then may that strength be given, for verily
Our strength is weakness, but His weakness strength!
To Him be glory evermore!
                    And so
Year One of this new era of my life
Is over. Oh to think that all this time
I might have been a dweller in the heavens!
That mansion in my Father's home above
Prepared for me, had not been vacant now!
And I had been with Christ, had seen His face,
The altogether lovely One, whom now
We see by faith alone, small faith at best.
One year, as we terrestrials measure time,
Out of that vast eternity of bliss,
In company with Him, and with His saints!
All peace, all joy, no stains of mortal sin!
All life's misunderstandings understood!
The tangled web unravelled—but alas!
This little world is still our dwelling-place.
When first I wakened from that tranquil sleep,
I dimly wondered if the gates of heaven
Had op'ed to let me in—it was not so!

continued

The voices round me spake in earthly tones,
And I was disillusioned; while as yet
Full sense was not restored, it seemed as though
Those gates were closed against me evermore;
And blank dismay possessed me, but, in truth,
My God had heard that scarcely-spoken cry,
And He preserved me. I had selfishly
Desired to put away the toils of life
Ere I had proved the armour He has given!
His will is best, and from my inmost soul
I would confess His wisdom, though the path
Be not of mine own choosing. Life or death,
Sorrow or joy, I take it thankfully,
And bless His Name therefor. I know not why
The promised rest is not for me as yet—
Perhaps my words, my actions, may be used
To point some needy one to Calvary,
Whose eyes are blinded by the Prince of Darkness.
Here, Lord, again I offer up myself
That Thine all-skilful Hand may mould this vessel,
And make it ever plastic for Thy use!
Oh, as my days, my years, pass one by one,
May all my opportunities be seized,
Regrets for failure growing ever fewer,
Until at length I join the choir of heaven,
Or hail most joyfully my Lord's return!

August, 1912

Old warrior-saint, thy warfare almost done,
    And glory shining from beyond the tomb,
(As when, cloud-hidden, the imperial sun
    Bursts with unconquer'd grandeur through the gloom),
With what high words of living, deathless hope,
    And tenderest depths of love, and solemn warning,
Thy letter charges us, (who dimly grope
    Through sunless night to the eternal morning),
As once it charged thy well-lov'd son in Christ,
    To watch, endure, shun evil, and be strong!
We say, "All earthly gain be sacrificed
    To do the right and overcome the wrong!"
But O the triumph! O the rich reward!
    For ever and for ever with the Lord!

March 3rd, 1913

Old warrior-saint

Frank always kept St. Paul before him as his great example, and often spoke from the epistles to Timothy when addressing young men in the ministry.

11 EASTER POEM

Methought I saw a vision of Death;
  His countenance was veil'd;
Like an arctic blast was his gasping breath,
  And he mutter'd, "I have fail'd!"
He sat beside an empty tomb,
  Cursing in bitter rage;
Light around him was changed to gloom,
  The gloom of sorrow and age.
"Sir," I said, (for I knew him not)
  "Whose is this tomb of stone?"
One scornful glance at my face he shot,
  And utter'd nought but a groan.
And then I look'd at his face in dread—
  It seemed so cold and grim.
"Thrice has He vanquished me," he said,
  "And I thought I had vanquish'd Him!
Thrice was I baulk'd of my rightful prey,
  Thrice He spoke, and I heard;
The bars I had made secure gave way—
  Burst at a single word!
Then I held Him for three short days—
  I thought my grasp was strong—
He is gone; and the legions of heaven raise
  A rapturous triumph-song!"
And, as I listened, I heard a sound
  Of angels praising their King;
For He, whom the chains of Death had bound,
  Waited to hear them sing.
They sang of His love, and the pains He bore,
  And how He had burst His prison;
And said, "The Maker whom we adore,
  The Son of God, is risen!"

March 21st, 1913

Methought I saw

Annotated, "Written by request".

12 A FRIEND

Sweet as the sweetest of musical harmonies,
  Sweet as the murmur of brooks without end,
Sweet as the breath of cool breezes in summer-time,
  Sweet—so sweet is the voice of a friend!

Better a world that the sun never shines upon,
  Infinite darkness, below and above,
Better a river bed desolate, waterless—
  Death is better than Life without Love!

Yet, O my friends, though the links I have forged for you,
  Burst with the straining of distance and time,
Yea, though my heart be a-hunger'd with loneliness,
  Life's dull clouds shutting out the sublime—

One Friend I have, who will always be true to me,
  Holding my hand when the sunlight is dim!
Oft have I griev'd Him, and slighted His tenderness,
  Oft been cold and disloyal to Him.

Still doth He dwell in the home I have offer'd Him;
  Though He be silent, His presence is bliss.
Think, O my soul! Thou art loved by the spotless One.
  Earth! thy sweetest is nothing to this!

April 8th, 1913

Sweet as the sweetest

Entered in Frank's manuscript book of poems; and published in *The Clarencian* in 1917.

13 TWO SONNETS

If I should die, and my immortal soul
   Should burst the barriers of its house of clay,
I doubt not but the solemn bells would toll
   And mourners weep along the churchyard way;
But oh! of all with whom my life is spent,
   Who pace along the selfsame path with me,
Who struggle daily with the same intent
   To follow Thee, O Christ, to follow Thee!
Will there be some who, after I am gone,
   Will feel a void within that none can fill,
Who, day by day, will gamely battle on,
   Yet, loving other men, will love me still?
Will wistfully recall the words I said,
   Speak in hush'd tones of me, when I am dead?

"Nay," says another voice, "is such thy love,
   That thou would'st have them mourn continually?
Thy friends, forsooth, must rate thy name above
   All other names, honour only thee?"
And I am worthless? Voice, thou speakest well;
   The truest love is selfless, and it lends,
Hoping for nothing; it disdains to tell
   If it receives in profit as it spends.
So let me pour it forth with lavish measure,
   And hush the yearnings of my lonely heart,
Draw from my soul its unrequited treasure
   Abundantly; that I, when I depart,
May, like the passing of a fragrant wind,
   Leave none but lovely memories behind.

June 7th–8th, 1913

If I should die

At nineteen Frank was thinking hard and setting the course of his life.

14 MY FRIEND

He was my friend; I saw his danger,
Watch'd how he left the narrow way;
I think I would have warn'd a stranger,
But to my friend I fear'd to say
What might offend, and, miserably weak,
Held back the words I fain would speak.

Aye, but the risk is daily greater,
And opportunities are few.
Being a lover, not a hater,
Whate'er the cost, I must be true.
Ere he is lost, I shall hold out my hand,
And draw him on to safer land.

So, pressing on and looking up, my friend
Shall reach along with me the journey's end!

June 12th, 1913

15 PEACE IN FAILURE

When, in the stillness of a summer eve,
  Thrill'd by sweet sadness of the setting sun,
I sit alone, and penitently grieve
  O'er all that I have done, and left undone—
All the sad waste of bygone years recalling,
  Good half-achiev'd, and evil undestroy'd,
To Him, who can preserve my feet from falling,
  I turn, and He is with me. Overjoy'd,
My spirit yearns with longing to behold
  His image, who, when tempted, never fail'd.
The past is pardon'd, and His arms enfold
  One who was faint, and left the heights unscal'd.
Long shadows flit around me; no stars shine,
  But all is light within me—He is mine!

May 25th, 1914

When in the stillness

While still at school Frank won a "first" in his external London B.A., in December 1913, and stayed on to work for a scholarship to the London College of Divinity (St. John's Hall, Highbury), which he entered in the autumn of 1914.

16 "WONDERFUL"

Isa. 9.6

There is an ignorance that none can feel
  But those who drink deep draughts from wisdom's well;
There is a wonder that is wont to steal
  Into their hearts like some enchanting spell.
Then with a wider vision they behold
  Marvels in earth and air and sky and sea,
And, baffled by the mysteries manifold
  Of life that is and life that is to be,
Some rest astonied; others, happier far,
  Add faith to knowledge and obtain firm grip
Of things unseen—their faith a fixéd star
  That guides the perilous journey of the ship.
These, from a full and overflowing heart
  Cry, "God in heaven, how Wonderful Thou art!"

1915

There is an ignorance
In his book of poems this one is dated April 7th, 1915. It was published in *The Clarencian* the same month.

17 BOYHOOD'S DREAMS

He stood, facing the sea:
And the wind that followed the flowing tide
And rocked the boats at the harbour's side,
Blew the soft hair from his forehead wide
And whispered, "Hark to me."

He saw how the sun, a burning red,
Plunged to its rest in the ocean bed,
And the furious clouds swept overhead,
Blood-hued, stormful and free!

The boy breathed deep and he listened long,
For strange was the wild wind's evensong,
And the music swelled to a chorus strong
That told of years to be.

He heard no words as the song swept by;
They were sung in a speech unknown and high,
But a glory-light was in his eye,
His face glowed wondrously.

And I knew, if his heart could have spoken then,
And told its thoughts in the ears of men
In a language not beyond their ken,
Such might their import be:

God of the earth, the winds, the sea,
Lord of the heavens above,
Thou who hast richly dowered me
With life and strength and love—

continued

Hardly I see and hardly read
  The future's hidden scroll,
Strange yearnings and new thoughts indeed
  Surge deep within my soul.

Visions of heights that I may climb,
  Grasping Thine own strong Hand,
Dreams of a great and glorious time
  When, hearing Thy command,

I shall spring gladly to the fight
  And grapple with the foe,
Behold the triumphing of right
  And wrong's last overthrow—

All this Thou knowest and canst see
  The wonder that is mine—
God who hast made and lovest me,
  Take me, and make me Thine!

Before 1915

He stood, facing the sea

Published in *The Clarencian* in the Winter Term, 1915, this poem was probably written when Frank was preparing to leave school in 1914.

18 NO LONGER SLAVES, BUT—FRIENDS

Let HIM take all! In His employ,
  His slave, I glory in my chains!
The load is light, the pain is joy,
  If Jesus reigns!

A bondman dare not claim rewards,
  Nor count his *all* a sacrifice.
My soul and body are the Lord's!
  He paid the price!

My Master! At His feet I lay,
  And vow'd to serve Him to the end,
Then—thrilling words!—I heard Him say
  "Not slave, but friend!"

Date uncertain, probably 1915–17

Let HIM take all

A poem based on John 15.15, "Henceforth I call you not servants; for the servant knoweth not what his lord doeth: but I have called you friends; for all things that I heard of my Father I have made known unto you."

MINISTER AND MISSIONARY

O thankless heart! O stubborn will!
I can resist His grace no more.
The Saviour's arms are open still,
He waits as heretofore—
Love triumphs—He shall have me.

Not only will the morning light
  Through shutter'd windows freshly stream,
  And wake us from this troubled dream,
But Christ is with us in the night!

Not only will that joy eclipse
  The sufferings of this present hour—
  O Joy in pain, in weakness Power,
Take *now* the offerings of our lips!

Now would we own Thou hast sufficed,
  Nor wait until the gloom is past—
  Should Day not dawn and darkness last,
Yet even now to live is Christ!

If, when the dimness of the night
  Hides half the beauty of His Face,
  He seems so fair, so full of grace—
What will He be in the morning light!

1917

Not only will the morning light

Frank was ordained on June 3rd, 1917, during the First World War, and became curate to St. Benedict's, Liverpool. His elder brother, Herbert, had already been killed at the Battle of the Somme, in July 1916, and when Frank wrote this poem he was meeting many in the parish with loved ones at the Front. In December 1928, when missionaries and Chinese Christians were suffering greatly from banditry, he printed it in *China's Millions*.

20 I TROD HIS EARTH

I trod His earth, I breath'd His air,
His sunshine gave me light and heat,
I owed my being to His care,
His goodness made life sweet—
All that I had He gave me.

I heard His clear, insistent Voice
Calling across the mad world's din;
I would not face the eternal choice—
"Thy Saviour—or thy sin"—
And yet He died to save me.

O thankless heart! O stubborn will!
I can resist His grace no more,
The Saviour's arms are open still,
He waits as heretofore—
Love triumphs—He shall have me.

1919

I trod His earth

In 1919 Frank moved to All Saints, Preston, and while there heard the call of God to service overseas. On April 29th, 1920, he offered himself to the China Inland Mission and sailed to China on November 10th, arriving in Shanghai on December 19th. (Intro., page 19.)

21 "BEHOLD, I HAVE TOLD YOU BEFORE"

Matt. 24.25.

There came to the gates of a citadel,
Garrison'd by the Lords of Hell,
  A Knight of the Cross,
He mark'd the turrets gloomy and tall,
He mark'd the strength of the massive wall,
  And, measuring gain and loss,
He turn'd away with a stifled sigh,
"*It is as I fear'd*—the walls are high,
  The battlements grim and grey.
How with a handful of weary men
  To face the Foe's array?
This is the hour of Satan's power,
  This is his day.
Oh that relief from across the sea
Might come in our sore extremity!
Lord, our weakness is known to Thee!"—
  He cried as he rode away.

There came another whose eager eye
Took stern note of the ramparts high,
  Of turret and wall.
His heart beat fast, for he knew full well
The strength of that lordly citadel,
  But he cried, "It shall surely fall!"
Why should we doubt or fear or fly?
IT IS AS HE SAID—the walls are high,
  We are few—but He overcame!
And we come in the Name of a living Lord,
  Today and for ever the same.
This is the hour of the Spirit's power,
  And here we claim—

continued

Clad in His armour, Faith our shield,
The Spirit's Sword in our hands to wield,
Sure that His glory shall be reveal'd—
  Victory through the Name!

1921

There came to the gates

At Chinkiang Frank joined in tract distribution in the streets, while still unable to speak the language. He was shocked by seeing the idolatry in a local temple—and also by the indulgent living of some missionaries. During this year he went to Wanhsien, Szechwan, and was deeply moved by the sight of the crowds of people, their superstition and the results of recent fighting. Moving to Liangshan he joined the mission school and met with nationalism among the schoolboys and sub-Christian standards among church members. "As little by little I begin to understand the problems of the work," he wrote, "the assurance that the battle is the Lord's . . . becomes of tremendous importance." (Intro., page 19.)

Ring'd around by Satan's power,
  Ceaselessly at grips with sin,
  Battle-stain'd and faint within—
'Father, save me from this hour!'

Nay—it was for this I came!
  Heard afar God's trumpet-call,
  Heard and answer'd, rose, left all—
'Father, glorify Thy Name!'

Thou, to whom this cry ascends
  From the death-strewn battle-line,
  On whose energy Divine
All our burning hope depends,

Hear, O Lord, Thy warrior's plea,
  Not that war should tamely cease,
  Not for some inglorious peace
Bringing shame on us—and Thee—

But for faith Thine aid to claim,
  Grace to struggle on nor tire,
  Deathless life and quenchless fire—
Father, glorify Thy Name!

1922

Ring'd around by Satan's power

Now in Suiting, Frank was again working among schoolboys. Because of the difficulties, he saw the danger of "settling down", and realized that he was not there as an observer "to see the country" but rather "sent by God to struggle even unto death". Invited to join the staff of the school for missionaries' children at Chefoo he declined, because he had been ordained to preach the gospel. (Intro., page 20.)

23 "WE LOVE HIM BECAUSE HE FIRST LOVED US"

1 John 4.19

I went forth to meet Him
 In the cool of the day,
With eager heart to greet Him
 As He passed on His way.
But I found Him there to greet me,
 Waiting till I came,
For HE had come to meet *me!*
 Oh, Love is His Name!

1923

I went forth to meet Him

Frequently called upon to travel through the beautiful Szechwan countryside, Frank wrote this meditation one early morning on the road, thinking no doubt of his tryst with God enjoyed before he started. (Intro., page 22.)

24 LORD OF OUR HEARTS

Lord of our hearts, Immanuel,
Who as at this time cam'st to dwell
Among us—
Here in a world that hated Thee,
Here where such woe awaited Thee,
Becoming Man—
No angel form of dazzling white,
Spotlessly pure and coldly bright,
Could win our love as Thou hast done,
God-begotten, yet Mary's Son!
Made like to us that we might be
Re-fashioned wholly, like to Thee—
We who have been to Calvary
And seen the Lord of glory die,
Who in Thy blood's most precious flow
All cleansing and all healing know,
May even now to Bethlehem go. . . .
Thy manger-bed, how dear to us,
For there Thou camest near to us,
  Lord of our hearts!

Lover of souls, we too would learn
  How to come *near* to men.
Thou it is who hast made us yearn
That these who serve vain gods may turn
  To Thee again.
But we are strangers from lands afar
And all unyielding the barriers are
  Holding us still apart.
Strange are our ways, our tongue, our race—
How may we find the secret place—
  This people's heart?

continued

Nothing, O Lord, have we withheld—
Love and labour—our heart's full store—
Still do we wait outside, repell'd,
While they but suffer us—no more!
What lack we yet? How to break through
This dull disguise of friendliness,
This outward form that veils the true,
Till our souls mingle and meet—no less!

O life! O death! Full life! grim death!
  We would not trifle with man's soul—
Our ransom'd being, every breath,
Our self, our life, yea, Lord, the whole
Is Thine—for we give it not by measure,
Bargaining not for woe or bliss,
Stripping ourselves of that or this
While ought remains of our richest treasure.
Thou gavest Life—in Thee we live—
The life Thou gavest us we give,
  Lord of our hearts!

December 1923

Lord of our hearts, Immanuel

After serious misunderstandings developed in the boys' school at Suiting, Frank faced discouragement by meeting many merely nominal Christians in the church. During this year Suiting was under the control first of the Christian General Feng Yü-hsiang and later of a bandit general who gave his men a free hand to loot. The unwelcoming attitude of many Chinese tested Frank severely but from the words of 1 Thess. 2.8 he drew comfort and the inspiration for this poem: "So being affectionately desirous of you, we were willing to have imparted unto you, not the gospel of God only, but also our own souls, because ye were dear unto us". (Intro., page 21.)

25 "AS ALWAYS, SO NOW ALSO"

Phil. 1.20.

One eager hope, one passionate desire,
One grand, all unifying aim—
Albeit in doubt's dark night or pain's fierce fire—
Let me bring glory to His Name!

"Always"—not only when to heedless ears
The gracious Voice sounds close beside,
But through the slow unfolding of the years,
Let Jesus Christ be magnified!

And since glib-tongued too lightly we aspire
In unconsidered prayer and vow,
Here in this hour, lest love's resolve should tire,
I pray, "As always, Lord, so now"!

1924

One eager hope

A poem written in the spring of 1924 after Frank came to the Paoning Theological College. When, in 1928, he became Editorial Secretary in London, his first leading article bore this title, expressing his own desire that God should be magnified. (*China's Millions,* March 1928.) (Intro., page 22.)

26 SONNET ON THE DEATH OF BISHOP AND MRS. CASSELS

We dare not grieve as others—if the Day
  Dawn'd suddenly for them, while Night's dark pall
  Shadows us still; and if a trumpet-call
Their warfare ended, summon'd them away,
While we fight on—shall we unthinking say
  That He, whose wisdom plann'd what should befall,
  Who to the end is Light and Lord of all,
Did not in *this* His changeless love display?
Till the Day dawn He lightens all our gloom,
  Till the fight cease, His banner leads us still;
  And we rejoice in His most perfect will,
Remembering how they labour'd, and for whom.

While as they two pass on to their reward,
On high and lifted up, we see—the LORD.

November 21st, 1925

We dare not grieve as others

In an epidemic of typhus many students of the theological college were taken ill and Bishop Cassels was infected when visiting one of them. Mrs. Cassels fell ill soon afterwards and both died. The double funeral provided an opportunity to preach the gospel to large numbers of officials and other non-Christians. (Intro., page 22.)

EDITOR

Was it His Voice that called?
Here, where the roads divide,
Faintly I hear the summons
Far up the mountain side. . . .

But, as I stood perplexed,
I heard the Voice close by—
His well-known Voice in the darkness—
"Follow, for it is I!"

27 THEY KNOW HIS VOICE

" . . . they know his voice . . . they know not the voice of strangers", John 10.4, 5

Was it His Voice that called?
  Here, where the roads divide,
Faintly I hear the summons
  Far up the mountain side.

This, I thought, was the road,
  Stretching for miles ahead,
That He, whose steps I follow,
  Surely meant me to tread.

That road is strange, untried.
  I should shrink back, appalled,
If it were any other
  Than His clear Voice that called.

But, as I stood perplexed,
  I heard the Voice close by—
His well-known Voice in the darkness—
  "Follow, for it is I!"

1927

Was it His Voice that called?

In 1926 the Theological College was temporarily closed on account of the political situation and high cost of living. The Houghtons were therefore granted furlough and travelled home via Siberia, hoping to return for the reopening. But anti-foreign feeling was increasing in China and during 1927 many missionaries were evacuated to the coast. For six months Frank assisted the Rev. Barclay Buxton in Tunbridge Wells, before becoming Editorial Secretary in London and resigning all hopes of returning to China. (Intro., page 23.)

He thwarted all
My fairest schemes,
Beyond recall
Banished my dreams.

Sadly resigned
To bear His Will,
I thought to find
Griefs sharper still.

But He, in love
No doubts could tire,
Gave Joy above
My heart's desire.

1928

He thwarted all

In the April 1928 number of *China's Millions* Frank's editorial was entitled "God our Trusted Leader". He wrote out of the personal experience of needing to trust and to follow in an apparent reversal of earlier guidance to China. (Intro., page 23.)

29 ROBBING GOD

We who would scorn to rob each other,
  Have we robbed Thee?
"All that is due you give your brother,
  Withholding Mine from Me."

Thou, who by pain beyond all telling
  Hast purchased me,
Freely I yield, Thy love compelling,
  All that is Thine to Thee.

1928

30 THE GREAT COMMISSION

"ALL the power" is given to Thee,
  "ALL the nations" are our field:
Thou hast pledged Thyself to be
  "ALL the days" our Strength and Shield.

1928

We who would scorn to rob each other

This poem was printed in the May 1928 issue of *China's Millions* with an editorial on the Macedonian church who "first gave their own selves to the Lord" (2 Cor. 8.5), and a reference to Mal. 3.8, "Will a man rob God? Yet ye have robbed me. But ye say, Wherein have we robbed thee?"

"All the power" is given to Thee

The annual meeting of the China Inland Mission in 1928 was addressed by the Rev. W. J. Southam on "Ownership—Claim—Presence" and this poem accompanied a report on the meeting in the June issue of *China's Millions.*

31 NOT ONE

Not one friend remained with Thee,
Jesus of Gethsemane,
When they came with stave and sword,
Traitor Judas at their head,
Men who owned Thee as their Lord
All abandoned Thee and fled.
Not one friend remained with Thee,
Jesus Christ, betrayed for me.

Not one voice was raised for Thee,
Jesus Christ of Calvary.
Faced by that tremendous choice,
All united in the cry,
Clamouring with insistent voice,
"Crucify Him! Crucify!"
Not one voice was raised for Thee,
Jesus, crucified for me.

Not one thing withheld from Thee!
This at length my vow shall be.
Only let me speak His praise
Whom the world condemned to die,
Following closer all my days
After Him whom men deny.
Not one thing withheld from Thee—
Jesus, living now in me!

1928

Not one friend remained with Thee

After a great missionary meeting at the Keswick Convention two hundred people rose to their feet to show their willingness to serve God overseas. It is thought that this poem was written after that event. *China's Millions* for September 1928 carried a leading article by Frank Houghton entitled "The Missionary Appeal" which gave impressions of the occasion.

32 LET THE FIRE BURN ON

Let the fire burn on in my heart, O LORD,
With a pure and cleansing flame—
Love from Calvary, power from Pentecost,
Zeal for Thy Holy Name.
Let the fire burn on!

1928

33 LOVING ME ALL THE TIME

Still He goes on loving me,
Loving me all the time.
I have wounded Him, His patience tried,
Spurned His tenderness, His Name denied,
But still He goes on loving me,
Loving me all the time.

1928

Let the fire burn on in my heart, O Lord

In December 1928 Frank's leading article in *China's Millions* was on "The Secret of Youth"; "though our outward man perish, yet the inward man is renewed day by day" (2 Cor. 4.16). "If we claim the daily inward renewal of life and power to which the apostle alludes," he wrote, "we shall remain fresh and virile, buoyant in our enthusiasm, fervent in our love. . . ." Forty-four years later he was still demonstrating the truth of his words. (Intro., page 23.)

Still He goes on loving me

This is one of a set of six choruses set to music. Others are to be found in the Appendix.

34 HE MUST REIGN

I want to see Thee triumphing
The whole world o'er,
The bounds of Thy dominion
Extending more and more,
Till all men know Thee,
And Thy glory see—
But now, LORD, while I wait Thy triumph,
Triumph Thou in me!

1929

I want to see Thee triumphing

By 1928 the anti-foreign tensions in China had diminished and new missionaries were again sent out. The following year the General Director issued the Call to Advance, with its appeal for two hundred new recruits. Frank put *China's Millions* to good use in supporting the challenge. At the CIM Swanwick Conference at Easter 1929 this chorus was sung to Frank's own tune. (Intro., page 24.)

35 WHEN I REMEMBER THEE

Trust that triumphs when fear dismays,
Light that shines in the darkest days,
Peace and power, and a song of praise!
  When I remember Thee.

1930

Trust that triumphs

It was soon apparent that the new advance was to be challenged by Satan, as missionaries in several provinces were taken captive and some were killed. Escorting a convoy of rafts with eleven missionaries down the Yellow River, Dr. George King was drowned, and Frank wrote and published a brief biography of him. He also edited the annual report under the title "We Wrestle", and wrote a leading article "The Enemy's Second Line of Defence", based on the words "That it spread no further" (Acts 4.17). *When I remember Thee* is characteristic of Frank Houghton's resilient spiritual response to such adverse circumstances.

THE UNFINISHED TASK

Facing a task unfinished,
  That drives us to our knees,
A need that, undiminished,
  Rebukes our slothful ease,
We, who rejoice to know Thee,
  Renew before Thy Throne
The solemn pledge we owe Thee
  To go and make Thee known.

Where other lords beside Thee
  Hold their unhindered sway,
Where forces that defied Thee
  Defy Thee still today.
With none to heed their crying
  For life, and love, and light,
Unnumbered souls are dying,
  And pass into the night.

We bear the torch that flaming
  Fell from the hands of those
Who gave their lives proclaiming
  That JESUS died and rose.
Ours is the same commission,
  The same glad message ours,
Fired by the same ambition,
  To Thee we yield our powers.

continued

O Father who sustained them,
   O Spirit who inspired,
Saviour, whose love constrained them
   To toil with zeal untired,
From cowardice defend us,
   From lethargy awake!
Forth on Thine errands send us
   To labour for Thy sake.

Facing a task unfinished

"A hymn of the Forward Movement" written for the annual meeting in May 1931 in support of the appeal for two hundred new missionaries. It has been included in new hymnals throughout the English-speaking world, to the tune *Aurelia*. (Intro., page 24.)

37 SINCERITY IN PRAYER

"Send forth more labourers!"
  —Praying so,
I heard the Master say,
"*Whom* shall I send, and who will go?"
And lo! I could not pray.

How can I plead that other men
  His harvesters may be
Till I have answered Him again,
  "Lord, here am I, send *me*"?

1931

"Send forth more labourers!"

Response to the appeal for the Two Hundred was not at first as great as was expected, and the faith of many was tested. In April 1931 Frank's leading article drew encouragement from the reply of Elijah's servant on Mt. Carmel. After Elijah with great faith had told Ahab to go and feast "for there is a sound of abundance of rain", the servant sent to look out to sea reported, "There is nothing" (1 Kings 18.43). To all appearances there was nothing, but faith still saw and soon received "abundance".

Landmarks along the track that lies behind
Have proved it is Thy custom to be kind—
Thou art the same today.
Yet with what freshness will Thy tender love
Surprise me on the hidden steeps above
As the mists clear away!

1931

Landmarks along the track

The advance was an uphill struggle against great odds all the way. The name Frank chose for the Annual Report was *The Steep Ascent*, and *Climbing* is the voice of faith anticipating the fulfilment. Before long, in November 1931, he was writing in *China's Millions* on Matt. 14.30, "beginning to sink", for funds were scarce and both the Communists and the Japanese were a danger in China. In his editorial, however, he wrote: "When men's hearts are failing them for fear, then 'look up' and 'lift up your heads'. No emergency has arisen or can arise to upset His calculations, on the contrary, each happening has not only been foreseen but must somehow serve the purposes of Him 'who worketh all things after the counsel of His own will!' " *Guard the Two Hundred* (No. 98) was another prayer in verse composed at this time. (Intro. page 25.)

39 ON FREDA'S DEATH

We do not ask Thee to explain
   Why Thou hast acted thus, nor how
Such seeming loss is turned to gain,
   Eternal gain—but even now,
Acknowledging that all Thy ways
Are right, we offer Thee our praise.

Others may count Thy dealings strange,
   That, with her service scarce begun,
Thy Voice should call her to exchange
   Great tasks for heaven's greater one,
But good is all that Thou hast planned—
We do not seek to understand.

We do not ask Thee to explain,
   We do not seek to understand,
We know He needed her again
   Who gave her, and at His right Hand
She shares His joy for evermore
Whom we in steadfast faith adore.

1932

We do not ask Thee to explain

How easily the question "Why?" could have been asked when Frank's sister Freda, who went to China in 1931 among the Two Hundred, fell ill and died after only ten months in the country. With this poem is a reference to Luke 10.21, "In that hour Jesus rejoiced in spirit, and said, I thank thee, O Father". (Intro., page 25.)

40 NO SURPRISE

"He himself knew what he would do", John 6.6

Was there ever a peril that found Thee unprepared,
  A need of flesh or spirit that Thou didst not foresee?
When darkness overwhelmed me, how should I have fared
  If the light and the darkness were not alike to Thee?

Plans of my wisest planning may come to nought, stillborn,
  Strange pathways lead me to where I would not be,
Yet if night gathers blackness when I thought to see the morn,
  The things that surprise me are no surprise to Thee.

Swift on the stroke that wounded, Thy healing Hand drew near,
  Thine arms were underneath me, around me, and above.
Mazed by new griefs undreamed of, how should I doubt or fear,
  Since the wonder of all wonders is Thine unfailing Love?

1933

Was there ever a peril

Funds were still short, famine was severe in China, the Communist army was menacing Szechwan, and in Sinkiang Percy Mather and Dr. Emil Fischbacher, the third of the Two Hundred to die, succumbed to typhus while attending wounded soldiers.

41 CAUSE THY FACE TO SHINE

Cause Thy Face to shine
That so its radiant light
May illumine mine,
However dark the night.

While they murmur, Who
Will shew us any good?
Keep me, lest I too
Yield to their faithless mood.

Thou, and only Thou,
Knowest Thy servant's case,
Lift upon me now
The shining of Thy Face.

1933

Cause Thy Face to shine

Personal perplexities and troubles were added to those of the Mission, but Frank found comfort in Ps. 80.3, "Turn us again, O God, and cause thy face to shine; and we shall be saved", and Ps. 4.6, "There be many that say, Who will show us any good? LORD, lift thou up the light of thy countenance upon us".

42 A PRAYER FOR EVERY DAY OF THE NEW YEAR

Give me new faith in the power of Thy Name,
New hope in Thy heartening Word.
Give me a heart that is newly aflame,
Aflame with Thy love, O Lord!

1933

Give me new faith

For six years Frank had been giving himself without stint to his editorial responsibilities and the work of the Mission. He had been reading in Deut. 1.6 and 2.3 God's words to Israel at Mount Horeb, "Ye have dwelt long enough in this mount", and at Mount Seir, eleven days' travel further on, "Ye have compassed this mountain long enough", and saw in them a warning of the danger of getting stagnant. The following year he spoke more than once at missionary conferences in China of the need to experience revival and quoted this poem in his address. (Intro., page 26.)

43 THE LINE IS CLEAR

My need was known
To Thee alone—
I called upon Thy Name
No other heard
Prayer's whispered word,
And yet the answer came.

Thus secretly,
'Twixt me and Thee,
Let traffic grow apace,
That even I
May testify
To Thine exceeding grace.

1934

My need was known

It was decided that Frank should revisit China to collect material for his book *China Calling* and to renew his impressions for editorial purposes. Gifts were received which made it possible for Dorothy to go with him, without cost to the Mission. When preparing for their journey they received a cheque, in answer to specific prayer, which exactly met their last remaining need. (Intro. page 25.)

44 THOU WHO WAST RICH

Thou who wast rich beyond all splendour,
  All for love's sake becamest poor;
Thrones for a manger didst surrender,
  Sapphire-paved courts for stable floor.
Thou who wast rich beyond all splendour,
  All for love's sake becamest poor.

Thou who art God beyond all praising,
  All for love's sake becamest Man;
Stooping so low, but sinners raising
  Heavenwards by Thine eternal plan.
Thou who art God beyond all praising,
  All for love's sake becamest Man.

Thou who art love beyond all telling,
  Saviour and King, we worship Thee.
Immanuel, within us dwelling,
  Make us what Thou wouldst have us be.
Thou who art love, beyond all telling,
  Saviour and King we worship Thee.

1934

Thou who wast rich

In December 1933 Frank's leading article in *China's Millions* was on 1 Cor. 9.19, "Though I be free from all men, yet have I made myself servant unto all, that I might gain the more", which he rendered in his title as "*I enslaved myself*". This, he pointed out, was the method our Lord Himself adopted as best to achieve His aims, "though he was rich, yet for your sakes he became poor". The ideas were already in his mind when he and Dorothy visited China, but it was while travelling through the mountains in Szechwan that the hymn took final form. It is sung to the tune *Fragrance*. A choir setting of this French carol melody is to be found in Christian Praise, No. 390. (Intro., page 26.)

45 GOD'S RESPONSE—AND MINE

In the night of my distress,
Utmost need and helplessness,
When I cried aloud to Thee,
"Here I am", Thou answeredst me.
(Isaiah 58.9)

Worlds created by Thy will
Wait Thy bidding to fulfil,
Lightnings flash from sea to sea—
"Here we are", they answer Thee!
(Job. 38.35)

What can I withhold from Thee,
Saviour who redeemedst me?
Where Thou callest, far or nigh,
Take me, use me; Here am I.
(Isaiah 6.8)

1935

In the night of my distress

While in Chengtu Frank was invited to become Bishop of East Szechwan and, as when faced with the prospect of never returning to China, he had found it difficult to accept without deliberate submission to the will of God, so now the magnitude of the task before him cast him again upon the Lord. He spoke at the 1936 Annual Meeting in London on this theme, challenging all true Christians to be ready for active service, saying, "Here am I!"

46 JOURNEYS IN CHINA

Along the road His wisdom planned,
He guides with strong and skilful Hand.
I walk secure with such a Guide
And rest is sure at eventide.

1934–35

47 A SECRET JOY

It is a secret joy
  To find
  The task assigned
Beyond our powers,
  For then if ought of good be wrought,
  Clearly the praise is His,
Not ours.

Along the road His wisdom planned

Travelling conditions were rough and unpredictable, and often neither vehicles nor lodgings could be relied upon. A sense of humour and great patience were needed. (Intro., page 26.)

It is a secret joy

Clearly Frank welcomed the pressure of the hand of God "strong upon" him as he effectively cast all his cares upon Him. (Intro., page 26.)

BISHOP

It is a secret joy
To find
The task assigned
Beyond our powers.
For then, if ought of good be wrought,
Clearly the praise is His,
Not ours.

48 WHITHER HE SENDS

Matt. 28.18–20

Whither He sends,
  To every place
    His power extends.

And every day,
  (Such is His grace),
    As we obey,

Till this world ends,
  He is pledged to stay
    With us, His friends.

1937

Whither He sends

Consecrated Bishop on January 25th, 1937, Frank Houghton embarked upon nearly four years of almost constant travel, difficulties, dangers and hard work. Having accepted the Lord's commission he now appropriated His promises and acted upon them. The disarming simplicity of this poem is the light contact of faith with the Source of Power by which he lived.

49 REVEAL THYSELF AGAIN

John 21.1

Reveal Thyself again!
The day is dawning on our weariness,
Our long night's labour and our ill-success—
Reveal Thyself again.

Is it enough that memory is stored
With hours most precious when we saw the Lord?
Reveal Thyself again.

O Love of yesterday, so strong, so near,
May we not count upon Thee now and here?
Reveal Thyself again.

1938

Reveal Thyself again!

The plodding toil of seemingly fruitless effort month after month, year after year, made the occasional conferences of missionaries like spiritual oases when fellowship and opportunity to "wait upon God" meant a great deal to everyone present. At one such conference at Chühsien in 1938 Bishop Houghton spoke on John 21.1, "Jesus showed himself again to the disciples . . ." after their fruitless night of self-effort, fishing—and stressed the constant need of renewal, of meeting the Lord again. (Intro., page 27.)

50 A HYMN OF PRAISE TO JESUS ENTHRONED

"We see Jesus . . . crowned with glory and honour", Heb. 2.9

Down in the darkest depths of shame
  My sinless Lord was found.
There on the cross He overcame,
  And now we see Him crowned,
  By faith we see Him crowned.

Weak to the scornful gaze of foes
  Who mocked His failing powers—
Yet by the might of God He rose,
  And now His strength is ours—
  His risen life is ours.

Jesus, who stooped from highest heaven
  To lift me to Thy side,
Honour and praise to Thee be given,
  For ever glorified—
  My Saviour, glorified.

1938

Down in the darkest depths of shame

This poem was sent to Bishop and Mrs. Houghton's friends on a printed greetings card "With warm greetings for Christmas and the New Year" from Chühsien, his diocesan centre in East Szechwan. (Intro., page 28.)

51 CHRISTMAS 1939

If in this strange eventful year—
Peace based uneasily on fear,
War that was madness, yet so near—
  We failed to prove Thee, Lord,
Yet now, when man's supremest skill,
His powers of feeling, thought and will,
Have failed to thwart the threatened ill,
  Shall we not prove Thee, Lord?
Is it in vain to seek Thy Face?
Rather, will not our desperate case
Provide a platform for Thy grace,
  That we may prove Thee, Lord?
Through storm and cloud Thy chariots speed,
We need the deepest depths of need
To prove Thy love is love indeed!

1939

If in this strange eventful year

Following the annexation of Czechoslovakia in 1938 an uneasy peace was agreed at Munich between Hitler and Great Britain. Preparations for war proceeded apace, however, and the invasion of Poland on September 1st, 1939, precipitated the "phoney" war which finally erupted and led to the evacuation at Dunkirk and the Battle of Britain. In China the Japanese invasion continued and more and more refugees from the east arrived in Szechwan, among them whole schools and universities. The Mission was feeling the pinch of enforced economies. But in it all Frank saw cause for thanksgiving, the occasion for proving the faithfulness, the grace and the love of God. (Intro., page 29.)

The thronging angels hailed His birth,
  Their chorus woke the morn.
But not for them He came to earth—
  "Unto us a Child is born!"

This wondrous Child is of our kin,
  Though Lord of earth and heaven,
Redeemer from the curse of sin—
  "Unto us a Son is given".

For God spared not His only Son,
  The Saviour freely came,
Endured until His work was done,
  For "Jesus" is His name!

We who have greater cause than they
  Acclaim with them the morn,
With angels and archangels say,
  Hallelujah! Christ is born!
  Hallelujah!

1939

The thronging angels hailed His birth

Printed with the music as "Greetings for 1959 from Bishop and Mrs. Houghton, St. Mark's Vicarage, Leamington Spa", this Christmas card bore the note: "The words of this carol—and the air—were written nearly twenty years ago as I walked, or rode in a sedan chair, over the hills of Szechwan in West China. I sent them to my brother Stanley . . . and he added the harmonies. In 1950 he joined 'the whole company of heaven' who 'with angels and archangels' laud and magnify that glorious Name. We of the Church Militant here on earth may join their Hallelujah Chorus in strains no less fervent because they are imperfect." (Intro., page 28.)

Their chants woke the [illegible];

19[illegible]9

GENERAL DIRECTOR

O Thou who dost direct my feet
To right or left where pathways part,
Wilt Thou not, faithful Paraclete,
Direct the journeying of my heart? . . .

This is the road of my desire—
Learning to love as God loves me,
Ready to pass through flood or fire
With Christ's unwearying constancy.

53 THE HEART'S JOURNEY

"The Lord direct your hearts into the love of God and into the steadfast endurance of Christ", 2 Thess. 3.5

O Thou who dost direct my feet
To right or left where pathways part,
Wilt Thou not, faithful Paraclete,
Direct the journeying of my heart?

Into the love of God, I pray,
Deeper and deeper let me press,
Exploring all along the way
Its secret strength and tenderness.

Into the steadfastness of One
Who patiently endured the cross,
Of Him who, though He were a Son,
Came to His crown through bitter loss.

This is the road of my desire—
Learning to love as God loves me,
Ready to pass through flood or fire
With Christ's unwearying constancy.

1940

O Thou who dost direct my feet

The Pacific War had not yet broken out and, although Shanghai was under Japanese occupation and control, the western allies had freedom of movement. Appointed General Director on October 21st, 1940, Bishop Houghton moved from Szechwan to Shanghai and this poem was printed there as a Christmas greeting, with Frank's rendering of 2 Thess. 3.5.

"Ready to pass through flood or fire"—prophetic words. But he and Mrs. Houghton were providentially out of the country when America and Britain became embroiled in war with Japan, or they would have been interned, immobilized. For them, instead, flood and fire involved many personal dangers and sufferings until World War II ended. This hymn is set to the tune *Cannock.* (Intro., page 28.)

54 I SLIPPED

"When I said, my foot slippeth; thy mercy, O Lord, held me up", Ps. 94.18

I slipped, and thought that none was nigh
To hear the echo of my cry.
And then, or e'er I was aware,
My Lord was there.

On that steep road, I might have known,
He would not leave me all alone.
Now, with His arm to lean upon,
I shall climb on.

How comforting to journey thus,
His mind directing both of us!
Great is my joy in Him, and He
Delights in me.

1940

I slipped, and thought that none was nigh

When D. E. Hoste succeeded Hudson Taylor as General Director he said, referring to his lonely position as leader, "Now there is no one but God!" The intimacy of Frank Houghton's fellowship with his Heavenly Father, like his faith, increased when he had no superior colleague to turn to.

55 THEN CAME JESUS

Then, when men's hearts were failing them for fear,
Then, when the forces of darkness were massed,
Then, as we wait with patient endurance—
He that shall come will come.

1940

56 FROM THEE IS ALL MY EXPECTATION, LORD

Rom. 8.31

From Thee is all my expectation, Lord,
O speak the word—
Thy servant waits for Thee.

1940

Then, when men's hearts were failing them for fear

"Then the same day at evening, being the first day of the week, when the doors were shut where the disciples were assembled for fear of the Jews, came Jesus and stood in the midst, and saith unto them, Peace be unto you", John 20.19. This was the time of Dunkirk and the Battle of Britain.

From Thee is all my expectation, Lord

Bearing the supreme responsibility for the leadership of many hundreds of missionaries, and having concern for even more Chinese pastors and lay-workers in the churches at such a time as this, Frank's faith looked in quiet confidence to Him whose work it was. (Intro., page 31.)

57 I HAVE A WEALTHY FATHER

I have a wealthy Father,
All the world's gold is His;
Far though the place, and late the hour,
Yet can His simple word of power
Meet my necessities.
His messengers, from sea to sea,
Wait His command to succour me!

1940

58 THOUGH EVERY ROAD WERE BARRED

No good will He withhold,
No evil can befall,
O faithless heart, be bold
To count on Him for all!

Though every road were barred,
Traffic with heaven is free,
And under angel guard
God's posts speed down to thee!

1940

I have a wealthy Father

It was God's ability to use any instrument, human or angelic, widow or raven, that Frank had in mind when he wrote these lines. Wartime stringencies only served to stimulate his confident trust in God. (Intro. page 31.)

No good will He withhold

Although, after the attack on Pearl Harbour in 1941, Free China was cut off from the outside world by practically every route except through Burma, and later only by air over "The Hump" from India, this poem written in December 1940 in fact reflects the interruption of mails and other communications at that time. But so long as communion with the Heavenly Father was possible no physical isolation mattered. (Intro., pages 32–33.)

59 THE EYES OF THE LORD

2 Chron. 16.9

Oh, let my heart be perfect with Thee,
  Like a clear pool, like a pure flame,
  Reflecting Thine image, adoring Thy Name—
So let my heart be perfect with Thee!

Shew Thyself strong, O Saviour, for me,
  Here where I need Thee, now when I cry,
  Thou on whose promise alone I rely—
Shew Thyself strong, O Saviour, for me!

1942

Oh, let my heart be perfect with Thee

Tremendous pressures bore down upon Frank in these grim war years. Responsibility for leadership of so large a Mission, with home bases in the United Kingdom, North America, South Africa and Australasia, and over a thousand missionaries and their children, included the care of many Germans and other continental associates. He also had to face great hazards from enemy action when travelling. Moreover Dorothy was usually with him, sharing the risks and hardships as she provided for his domestic needs. No wonder his heart cried out to God when he read 2 Chron. 16.9, "the eyes of the Lord run to and fro throughout the whole earth, to shew himself strong in the behalf of them whose heart is perfect toward him". This was the Scripture committed to him by his father as the train pulled away from the platform on Frank's first departure for China, and constantly borne in mind through the years.

Through men whom worldlings count as fools,
Chosen of God, and not of man,
Reared in Thy secret training schools,
Moves forward Thine eternal plan.

And now, though hidden from our ken
In Midian desert, Sinai's hill,
Spirit of God, Thou hast Thy men
Waiting Thy time to do Thy will.

When blazing out upon our night
Flashes the Pentecostal flame,
May I be found with heart alight,
Burning to magnify Thy Name.

Not as Thy prophets who declare
The Word that thousands hear and own,
If I may have the smallest share
In setting Christ upon His Throne.

1943

Through men whom worldlings count as fools

Safely at their destination, Chungking, after many months of hazardous travelling by sea, land and air, it is understandable if Bishop Houghton relaxed into almost gay optimism and confidence. The outcome of the war was still far from certain and setbacks were frequent; funds were often in short supply and exchange rates disadvantageous, but the work of God was moving forward and the God of Moses and of Elijah was his own God. When missionaries volunteered for military service the consular authorities advised them to continue their work for China, but to many critics all missionary work was a waste of time. To Frank Houghton all pioneer advances came as an encouragement, for he longed to see the cross uplifted and Christ made known wherever Christless men were to be found. (Intro., page 33.)

61 WHAT SHALL I DO?

What shall I do when the brook runs dry,
  And the ravens come no more?
Thy Father God, who reigns on high,
Thy utmost need can still supply
  From His exhaustless store.

1943

What shall I do when the brook runs dry . . . ?

This gem of faith comes from the days when the Mission in Free China was beleaguered and living to all appearances "precariously", like Elijah by the brook Cherith. Soon afterwards a favourable financial exchange rate was negotiated and the Treasurer of the CIM was appointed to handle funds for all missions in Free China. (Intro., page 33–34.)

62 BY THY COMMAND

By Thy command our table has been spread,
From Thy dear Hand we take our daily bread
And, grateful, give the offering of our praise
Henceforth to live and serve Thee all our days.

October 1943

63 FOR THY DAILY MERCIES

For Thy daily mercies
Be Thy Name adored—
More than all we praise Thee
For Thyself, O Lord!

1944–45

By Thy command our table has been spread
For Thy daily mercies

Communal meals at the wartime headquarters in Chungking often began with a song of thanksgiving, of which these are examples.

64 EBENEZER—JEHOVAH JIREH

EBENEZER—Hitherto hath the LORD helped us
How plain and clear
The steps appear
By which my Father led me here!
The road is bright
With sunset light,
Which mists of morning hid from sight.

JEHOVAH JIREH—The LORD will provide
And since Thy Hand
My day has planned,
How can I fail to understand
That to the end
I may depend
Unquestioning on Thee, my Friend!

1945

How plain and clear

For decades the Mission had drawn inspiration from the association of the name given in 1 Sam. 7.12, to the stone set up by Samuel to testify, "Hitherto hath the LORD helped us", with the name in Gen. 22.14 (marginal reading), used by Abraham after offering the substitute ram, "The LORD will provide". In 1945 the General Director's message to the Mission was one of encouragement from a similar passage, Deut. 3.21, "Thine eyes have seen all that the LORD your God hath done. . . . So shall the LORD do . . .", and these verses accompanied it. (Intro., page 34.)

65 HIS RESOURCES

When I think of my Father's eternal design,
By which His resources are mine;
When I think of the wealth in the heavenly mint
On which I may draw without stint;
When I think what my Father is planning to do,
There's NOTHING too GOOD to be TRUE!

1946

When I think of my Father's eternal design

The unchanging boyishness in Frank Houghton endeared him to his friends and made him popular with the young. Bishop and General Director he might be, but the natural way for him to express his strong faith, hope and love was sometimes in an almost jocular jingle, like this one of which the words and air were composed together. It was intended to be sung. In 1950 he sent it, complete with musical score, to his many friends as a Christmas greeting, with this note: "I have chosen this chorus for our greeting this year because my brother Stanley, who went to be with Christ on July 17th, 1950, added much to its value by supplying sturdy harmonies to my words and air. He is now experiencing the truth of the words in a greater degree than is possible for us at present. . . ." (Intro., page 35.)

66 STAR WHOSE LIGHT SHINES O'ER ME

Star whose light shines o'er me,
  Rock on which I stand,
Guide who goes before me
  To my fatherland,
Daily bread reviving,
  Spring that cheers my heart,
Goal to which I'm striving—
  All, O Lord, Thou art!

But for Thine upholding
  Where would strength be found?
By Thy arms enfolding
  Thou dost gird me round.
Faith—a shining beacon—
  Hope, lest I lose heart—
Love that cannot weaken—
  All, O Lord, Thou art!

So from morn till even
  By Thy help I come,
Till the bells of heaven
  Ring my welcome Home.
Then new songs I'll sing Thee
  From a joyful heart.
Naught have I to bring Thee—
  All, O Lord, Thou art!

1948

Star whose light shines o'er me

Lord Jesus Christ, the work is Thine (No. 67)

These two translations from the German, with the help of Hans M. Wilhelm, son of a member of the Marburger Mission, have enriched our hymnary. The tune to which the first is set was by Minna Koch (1845–1924) and that of the second by J. Gersbach, annotated Karlsruhe, 1822. *Star whose light shines o'er me* is in the 1962 edition of the Baptist Hymnal, and *The Work is Thine* in several other books. (Intro., page 36.)

67 THE WORK IS THINE

Lord Jesus Christ, the work is Thine;
Not ours, but Thine alone;
And prospered by Thy power divine
Can ne'er be overthrown.
Before it pushes to the light
The corn of wheat is hid from sight.
Deep in the silent earth it lies,
Its very self decays and dies,
Decays and dies,
Losing itself it dies.

To glory Thou didst rise through pain,
Jesus, our risen Head,
And all who follow in Thy train
The selfsame path must tread.
So in Thy fellowship we go,
Refusing not to share Thy woe,
If only Thou dost lead us through
The gate of death to Life anew,
To Life anew,
Through death to Life anew.

Thou as a corn of wheat didst die
And sink into the grave.
Now quicken, Fount of Life, we cry,
The dead Thou cam'st to save!
O send Thy heralds everywhere
The tidings of Thy Name to bear
And, till its fame is fully shown,
We pledge ourselves to make it known,
Thy Name alone,
We live to make it known!

1948

See note on page 127

68 THIS IS THE TIME TO TRUST

When the roads now blocked are clear and free,
When the doors fast barred swing open wide,
I shall be glad that I trusted Thee,
That through long, grey days of uncertainty
I never questioned Thy love to me,
Thy Name was glorified!

1949

When the roads now blocked

The key to understanding this poem is the phrase "long, grey days of uncertainty". After the end of World War II new hope of advance on all missionary fronts seemed justified, and in spite of setbacks the title Frank chose for a leading article was Attack: "It may be that the LORD will work for us" (1 Sam. 14.6). Soon, however, as the red hand of merciless Communism took tighter and tighter hold of the people of China, and the possibility of continuing missionary work became less and less, there was little the General Director could do than to hold on in blind faith. The very safety of his missionaries was in question. Some were to be arrested and to face serious charges. His comfort was in the promises of God. In a cable expressing sympathy J. O. Sanders, who later succeeded Frank as General Director, quoted Isa. 45.2, "I will go before thee, and make the crooked places straight: I will break in pieces the gates of brass and cut in sunder the bars of iron"—words which, together with Ps. 62.5, "My expectation is from him", appear to have inspired this poem, a personal declaration of faith.

69 KNOWING THEE I CANNOT DOUBT

Knowing Thee, I cannot doubt
Thou wilt guard my "going out",
And my "coming in" shall be
As and when it pleaseth Thee.

1949

Knowing Thee, I cannot doubt

A little heart-song on reading Ps. 121.8, "The Lord shall preserve thy going out and thy coming in from this time forth, and even for evermore".

70 WHEN GOD IS SILENT

When God is silent for a space,
And when thick darkness veils His face,
Until I hear His voice once more,
Until I see Him as of yore,
On this firm ground my feet are set—
His promise, "I WILL NOT FORGET".

1949

When God is silent

A companion meditation on Isa. 49.15, "Can a woman forget her sucking child . . .? Yea, they may forget, yet will I not forget thee."

Note on poems 69 and 70

These two poems appear on the same sheet of paper as "This is the time to trust", apparently typed in Shanghai in 1949. With them are some notes entitled "De Profundis", "The Ground of our Confidence", and "Faith's Opportunity", which continue: "Do you see NO glimmer of light on the horizon, NO rift in the clouds? Then this is emphatically the time for faith. Like Abraham we do not stagger at the promises of God through unbelief, but are strong in faith, giving glory to God.

A faith that shines more bright and clear
When tempests rage without,
That when in danger knows no fear,
In darkness feels no doubt.

'Said I not unto thee, that if thou wouldest BELIEVE, thou shouldest see the glory of God?' John 11.40." (Intro., page 36.)

71 THE THICK DARKNESS

I thought I was walking all alone
  Into darkness immense and drear.
But where it was densest a Hand touched my own,
  And a Voice spoke, gentle and clear:
"Do you not think you might have known
  That I should be here?
Your need is met, your way will be shown,
  Be of good cheer!"

1951

I thought I was walking all alone

"For various reasons 1951 was not an easy year for me," Frank wrote in gross understatement of perhaps the most shattering year of his life. The Mission had had to withdraw bodily from China, a few of the missionaries remained in custody and the future was unknown. Yet God spoke to him in the clarity of a vision, and this poem is the voice of confidence. The thick darkness was darkness "*where God was*" (Exod. 20.21), and in it Frank remembered the words of Solomon, "The LORD said that he would dwell in the thick darkness" (1 Kings 8.12), and of Isaiah, "Who is among you that feareth the LORD, that obeyeth the voice of his servant, that walketh in darkness, and hath no light? let him trust in the name of the LORD, and stay upon his God" (Isa. 50.10). So he commented, "It does matter . . . that *in* all our trials and testings we should be more than conquerors. . . ." He loved to speak on 2 Tim. 4.16, 17: "At my first answer no man stood with me. . . . Notwithstanding the LORD stood with me, and strengthened me . . ." (Intro., page 39.)

THE LAST TWENTY YEARS

Dark and dim is the way ahead—
"How can I plan for the journey?" I said.

"Did you not know, on the way ahead
I am planning for you?" the Master said.

72 TASTE AND SEE

"O taste, and see, how gracious the Lord is: blessed is the man that trusteth in him", Ps. 34.8 (Prayer Book Version)

We taste and we are satisfied,
   Yet hunger still for more,
And long that all men, far and wide,
   May share in God's rich store.

1953

We taste and we are satisfied

The first recorded verse from this period of his life, "Taste and See", followed five happy months in India, working on the biography of Amy Carmichael of Dohnavur, and voices Frank's longing that all the world should experience the goodness of the Lord.

73 THE ANSWER OF GOD

As bright hopes faded, stair by stair
Down plunged the prophet to despair.
His people cruelly misused,
Their claim for liberty refused,
Hard words from Pharaoh, and—far worse—
The whip-lash of his people's curse.
And, in his hour of utmost need,
God had done nothing, paid no heed . . .
Then like a flash God's Word broke through,
"Now shalt thou see what I will do".

Does the dark cloud engulfing you
Seem dense as ever Moses knew?
Ev'n the next step is hid from view?
All props are knocked from under you,
Your plans have failed, your courage too,
There is nought left that you can do?
On the last rung of the steep stair
That leads straight downward to despair,
This is the Word of God to you,
"NOW SHALT THOU SEE WHAT I WILL DO."

1953

As bright hopes faded

This poem could well have been written in 1951, but it was in fact the cry of the man of faith battling once again as he had battled in the sea at Boscombe, forty-two years earlier, to stay alive and not go down under the waves. New discouragements reminded him of testings experienced in the past, and of the loving kindness of the Lord. As Moses turned to Him asking, "Why is it that thou hast sent me?"—when Pharaoh's anger was added to Israel's burdens and God's people blamed Moses—and God answered, "*Now shalt thou see what I will do* to Pharaoh" (Exod. 5.20–6.1), so now Frank Houghton held firmly to this lifeline. It is more a song of triumph than of struggle. (Intro., page 40.)

74 DEDICATION OF THE NEW VICARAGE FOR ST. MARK'S

Hallow this house, O Lord, we pray,
And let it ever be
Kept by Thy grace a sacred place
Where we may meet with Thee.

Let all who enter by this door,
And all within who dwell,
Be made aware that Thou art there,
Our Lord, Immanuel.

This gift of Thine we now commit
To Thy protecting care,
And with one voice and heart rejoice
That Thou hast answered prayer.

1955

Hallow this house

After three years in a rented house and many difficulties surmounted in answer to believing prayer, the new vicarage of St. Mark's was dedicated to the service of God. This hymn was sung outside the house at its formal opening. (Intro., page 40.)

75 SUCCESS AND FAILURE

Why do we fail, while Satan everywhere
  Extends his sway?
Why are we baffled, almost in despair
  To find the way?
"This kind comes forth by nothing but by prayer"—
  Teach us to pray!

By prayer we turn the battle to the gate,
  The foe gives ground.
Captives are rescued from their helpless state,
  The lost are found.
By prayer we work, and joyfully await
  The trumpet's sound!

1956

Why do we fail?

In preparation for an evangelistic mission at St. Mark's, Leamington, in 1956, led by the Rev. R. C. Lucas and a team of students, Bishop Houghton printed these verses on cards to encourage and guide prayer support for the venture. The first verse was sub-titled, The Reason for Failure, and the second, The Secret of Success. As always, it was in the face of challenge that his strongest lines were written.

76 "MY GOD SHALL SUPPLY ALL YOUR NEED"

Phil. 4.19

Since on His promise I rely
That God will all my need supply,
The inference is clear indeed—
What God withholds I do not need.
So, with His goodness satisfied,
I rest, nor ask for aught beside.

1957

Since on His promise I rely

The life of faith was not restricted to the field of foreign missions. Faced with extensive repairs to the church roof, at a cost of thousands of pounds, the vicar declined to draw from church funds while other commitments remained unmet. "Since on His promise I rely" was his *credo* at this time, the promise he had in mind being the words of the title.

77 WAITING

"Wait, I say, on the LORD", Ps. 27.14

Waiting, if He bids me wait,
  Is not time ill-spent,
Let His call come soon or late—
  I shall be content.

Only, when He beckons me
  To a task undone,
Let my eyes be swift to see,
  And my feet to run!

1957

Waiting, if He bids me wait

Again, the simplicity of this poem could deceive, but as a sermon on patience it is profound—like some of the Psalmist's disarmingly simple statements:

"Wait on the LORD: be of good courage, and he shall strengthen thine heart: wait, I say, on the LORD" (Ps. 27.14).

The care of the shepherdless congregation at Drayton was the "task undone" to which the Lord was beckoning. (Intro., page 41.)

78 MY FATHER HAS A REST-HOUSE

My Father has a rest-house
  Round every turn in the road,
Wherein the weary pilgrim
  May lay aside his load,
And there enjoy refreshment free
In his own Master's company.

Thus strengthened, on he journeys
  Steadfast and of good cheer,
Praising the Lord whose kindness
  Provides such lodging here . . .
Yet to no lodging will he come
That he can e'er mistake for Home.

1960

My Father has a rest-house

In 1960 a country rectory with beautiful views became Bishop and Mrs. Houghton's happy "rest-house" for the next three and a half years. (Intro., page 41.)

79 MY LORD, WHO IN THE DESERT FED

My Lord, who in the desert fed
On soul-sustaining heavenly Bread,
Words that were meat and drink to Thee—
O let them daily nourish me!

And since the sword that served Thee well
In battling with the powers of hell
Is even now at hand for me,
Help me to wield it manfully.

But first, O holy, gracious Lord,
I pray Thee, let Thy Spirit's sword
Pierce heart and conscience, till I see
Both what I am and ought to be.

Thy Word my rule—and my delight,
My strength for service and for fight!
For this exhaustless treasure-store,
My Lord, I praise Thee and adore!

1961

My Lord, who in the desert fed

In 1911 when he was seventeen Frank wrote a sonnet for the tercentenary of the Authorized Version of the Bible (No. 6). Now, fifty years later, he composed this hymn and suggested as suitable tunes: *Deus Tuorum Militum, Truro* or *Wareham* (*Christian Praise*, 291). A Scripture Union card signed by his mother in 1900, when Frank was six, was kept in his Bible all his life. He maintained his link with the "S.U." and read the chosen passage each day. (Intro., page 41.)

With tenderest tokens of Thy love
My every day is blest;
Yet for this Day, all days above,
Thou dost reserve Thy best.

Sacred are all my days to me,
For all my days are Thine;
Yet Thou hast chosen this to be
'Twixt me and Thee a sign.

So midst the whirl of six days flown
And six days' whirl to be,
The Day that Thou hast called Thine own
Is pure delight to me.

Give holy quietness today,
Peace with the morning dew,
And, as the daylight wears away,
Lord, show Thyself anew!

1962

With tenderest tokens of Thy love

Written at Drayton, this hymn was shared with the Houghtons' friends through their personal Christmas card for 1962, and bore these references to Scripture: Isa. 58.13, 14, Rev. 1.10 and Ezek. 20.20. "Hallow my sabbaths; and they shall be a sign between me and you, that ye may know that I am the LORD your God." The "Lord's Day", as he loved to call it, was always a "pure delight" to him. The tune *Belmont* was suggested for this hymn. (Intro., page 41.)

81 IF I HAD LEFT THE PATHWAY OF THY WILL

"I being in the way, the LORD led me", Gen. 24.27

If I had left the pathway of Thy will,
Ignoring warnings that were clear and plain,
Thy mercy would have followed me, until
My careless feet had found the road again.

But better far if, being in the way,
I followed where the signals pointed me,
And by Thy guidance, at the close of day,
Found shelter in the place prepared by Thee.

1963

If I had left the pathway

Having followed the leading of God to Parkstone, Poole, it was no surprise to find, when house-hunting began, that the first flat visited was the one He had prepared for them, with a kind and helpful landlady. (Intro., page 41.)

82 THE JOY OF THE BRIDEGROOM'S FRIEND

Knowing Thee, Lord, it is my chief desire
  Daily to know Thee more and more,
And then to introduce my friends, and see
Thy mighty love attracting them to Thee,
  While I stand silent, and adore.

1964

Knowing Thee, Lord

This meditation before an evangelistic campaign at Parkstone was prompted by John 3.29, "It is the bridegroom to whom the bride belongs. The bridegroom's friend who stands by and listens to him is overjoyed at hearing the bridegroom's voice. This joy, this perfect joy, is now mine. As he grows greater I must grow less" (NEB). As the first opportunity to play a significant part in such an activity since relinquishing parishes of his own, this occasion was a great joy to Frank.

83 WHAT SHALL I RENDER?

"What shall I render unto the LORD for all his benefits toward me?"
Ps. 116.12

God, to whom I owe
   Life and breath and all things,

Son of God, who loved me,
   And gave Himself for me,

Holy Spirit, within me,
   Guiding, directing me,
   Making my heart His home—

I must care for others
   As God cares for me,

I must love as Christ loves,
   Freely, selflessly—

Yes, and the Spirit's fire
   Must be aflame in me—
O let the fire burn on!

1965

God to whom I owe

With the completion of the centennial book, *The Fire Burns On,* all that remained was to give thanks and an offering of praise which found expression in these lines. (Intro., page 42.)

Treading the same steep path our fathers trod,
  In glad obedience and with hearts aflame,
We sing the praises of our faithful God,
  Advancing still in Jesus' conquering Name.

Through the long years that Name has been made known
  To countless thousands who had never heard,
And, by the Spirit's mighty power alone,
  Hearts have been opened to the pardoning Word.

The Builder of Thy Church, O Lord, art Thou,
  And Thou the Shepherd who the flock dost keep,
Let living stones be added even now,
  And by Thy loving Hand protect Thy sheep.

It is Thy Hand, O Lord, that beckons still,
  Thy Voice that calls, and cannot be denied,
Only give grace and strength to do Thy will,
  And let Thy Name alone be glorified!

So let the fire burn on, until its blaze
  Lightens the darkest fastnesses of sin,
And Thou, who hast been with us all the days,
  Shalt come again to bring Thy kingdom in!

1965

Treading the same steep path

A Centennial Hymn. In 1865 Hudson Taylor founded the China Inland Mission. For a hundred years the faithfulness of God had not failed the Mission or its individual members. To the anthology of prose and verse which he edited to commemorate the Centenary, under the title *The Fire Burns On*, Frank Houghton contributed this hymn, with sub-titles for each verse: i. Our faithful God; ii. The work in China; iii. Prayer for China; iv. Along new trails; v. The fire burns on. Tunes recommended were *Farley Castle* and *Ellers*. (Intro., page 42.)

85 THE ROAD AHEAD

"Jesus said . . . I am the way", John 14.6

Dark and dim is the road ahead—
"How can I plan for the journey?" I said.

"Did you not know, on the road ahead,
I'm planning for you?" the Master said.

1966

Dark and dim is the road ahead

During forty-three years of married life the Houghtons had never been able to settle in the same home for longer than three or four years, with the one exception of Leamington, five years. Now, when the time came to move once more, the Lord had planned a convenient flat for them where they made a happy home for the final five years in service together for Him. This and the following poems give an insight into his mind and soul during the years at Parkstone. (Intro., page 42.)

Conscious of weakness, I may claim
Strength that is promised in Thy Name.
Let the world's turmoil still increase—
In Thee, my Saviour, there is *peace*.
Above the raging storms I hear
Thy clear, strong voice, "BE OF GOOD CHEER!"

probably 1967

Conscious of weakness, I may claim

Ps. 29.11, "The LORD will give *strength* unto his people; the LORD will bless his people with peace", was one of Frank's favourite verses. The year 1967 had in many ways been difficult, but the Word of God continued to give the needed fortitude:

"My grace is sufficient for thee: for my *strength* is made perfect in weakness" (2 Cor. 12.9).

"These things I have spoken unto you, that in me ye might have peace. In the world ye shall have tribulation: but be of good cheer; I have overcome the world" (John 16.33).

87 THE CHALLENGE

Father, we come before Thy throne,
 Ready to hearken and obey
The clear commands of Christ alone,
 Thy Son, the Life, the Truth, the Way.

Where doors are open, give us grace
 To enter with the Spirit's sword,
There to proclaim in every place
 The saving Name of Christ the Lord.

Should doors be barred—in simple trust
 Alert we wait the trumpet call,
And follow Christ because we must—
 His mighty love constrains us all.

So in the challenge of this hour
 Thy servants worship and adore!
Thine is the kingdom, Thine the power,
 And Thine the glory evermore!

1969

Father, we come before Thy throne

Twenty years had passed since the Communists overran China, and the prospects of liberty for the gospel to be freely declared to her people were no brighter than at that time. Frank was now seventy-five, yet in this poem the fire of his early missionary spirit remains unabated. He wrote this hymn for the Mission's annual meeting on May 13th, 1969.

88 SHOW ME THY GLORY

Show me Thy glory, Lord,
   In this new year.
Break through the darkness, Lord,
   In splendour clear.
Speak to me face to face,
   As friend to friend,
Show me Thy glory, Lord,
   To the year's end!

1970

Show me Thy glory, Lord

Some signs of failing health now cast Frank and Dorothy on the comfort of the Lord, but as he read Exod. 33, the verses 11 and 18 were God's word to him:

"The LORD spake unto Moses face to face, as a man speaketh unto his friend", and "I beseech thee, show me thy glory".

He did not know that this prayer for the new year was to be fulfilled so completely or so soon. He saw the year through but in January 1972 his fight of faith was seen to be reaching its end. As he lay dying he listened to the Hallelujah Chorus from Handel's "Messiah", and the last word Frank was heard to speak was the word "Wonderful!" (Intro., page 43.)

APPENDIX

APPENDIX

89 THE TWO STREAMS

Going our several ways apart,
  Dreaming our several dreams,
With a wall dividing heart from heart
  Like two parallel streams—
One where the smiling sun has shone,
  Kissing its rippling flow;
One that the shadows dwell upon,
  Where trees of the graveyard grow . . .

The wall fell down with a sudden crash,
  The streams were merged in one:
There came to me one thought like a flash,
  "Now then, what of the sun?"

1915

90 CHINA'S BOYS AND GIRLS

China's boys and girls, in millions over the sea,
Living and growing, working and playing,
just like you and me.
Living and growing, yet never knowing
Jesus who died to save—
On through life without Him, down to a Christless grave.
Saviour, help me to feel it, help me to work and pray.
  If Thou art calling me to go—I am ready, Lord, to obey!

1928

91 "NOT FOR OURS ONLY"

"Not for ours only"—in His love divine
Jesus suffered for our sins—yours and mine.
But these glad tidings all the world must share—
Jesus died for sinners—ev'rywhere!

92 CONSTRAINING LOVE

Christ's love constrains me,
I must henceforth be
His who gave His life's blood
Freely for me.

1928

93 THE BOND DIVINE

Whether I wake or sleep,
Whether I live or die,
I am Christ's and Christ is mine,
And nothing can sever the bond Divine,
Eternally!

1928

94 SINS THAT ARE PAST

Sins that are past would condemn me,
Sin of today would enslave,
But Christ on the Cross made atonement,
And Jesus is living to save!

1928

95 THE LIFE OF GOD

Full to overflowing may we ever be,
Living waters welling up continually!
That the blessing may abound
To the thirsty all around,
Full to overflowing with the Life of God!

1928

96 THE NEW DAY DAWNS

The new day dawns, Thou art my Guide.
Show me Thy way, protect, provide.
  O let me be of use to Thee!
That Jesus may be glorified.

1930

97 APPEAL FOR THE TWO HUNDRED

Lord, by the call of China's need,
  And by the love of Calvary,
Choose and send forth, we humbly plead,
  Two hundred witnesses for Thee.

1929

98 GUARD THE TWO HUNDRED

Guard the Two Hundred! LORD, we claim
Moment by moment, hour by hour,
In CHRIST our Saviour's conquering Name
A victory over Satan's power!

Use the Two Hundred, LORD, we plead,
That, girded with Thy Spirit's sword,
They may advance where Thou dost lead
And win fresh trophies for their LORD.

1931

99 OVER-BURDENED, FAINT, DISHEARTENED

Over-burdened, faint, disheartened,
Tempted to despair?
Look to Jesus, He is strong to help you,
He answers prayer.

1931

100 FULNESS OF LIFE

Fulness of life, and wealth, and power,
All is CHRIST's by the Father's dower.
Yet in His grace abundant and free
He's willing to share it all with me—
To share it all with me.

1931

INDEX OF TITLES AND FIRST LINES

The words and music of the poems indicated by (M) are available in a booklet entitled TEN TUNES *by the Rt. Rev* FRANK HOUGHTON, *obtainable from the Publications Manager, Overseas Missionary Fellowship, Newington Green, London, N16 9QD*